A
MAN - GOD
NAMED
JESUS

Covenant Blessed Ministries, LLC
A Man / God Named Jesus
An Interview with Jesus
Web: Godnamedjesus.com
Web:covenantblessedministries.com
E-mail: godnamedJesus.com@gmail.com

A
MAN - GOD
NAMED
JESUS

An Interview With Jesus

INDI FRATARCANGELO-KIMSEY

TATE PUBLISHING
AND **ENTERPRISES**, LLC

Published by Tate Publishing & Enterprises, LLC
127 E. Trade Center Terrace | Mustang, Oklahoma 73064 USA
1.888.361.9473 | www.tatepublishing.com

Tate Publishing is committed to excellence in the publishing industry. The company reflects the philosophy established by the founders, based on Psalm 68:11,
"The Lord gave the word and great was the company of those who published it."

Book design copyright © 2013 by Tate Publishing, LLC. All rights reserved.
Cover design by Rtor Maghuyop
Interior design by Jomel Pepito

Published in the United States of America

ISBN: 978-1-62902-085-3
1. Religion / General
2. Religion / Christian Life / General
13.10.21

My dedication is to God's laborers for His harvest. You don't always see what your labor produces, but the Lord does.

Ministering one day to a woman in jail, we were talking of God's word and His love and the promises He has for all of us. A young lady looked at me in astonishment and said "God said that? Did He tell you I was going to be ok? And He will be with me?" Those words reached down deep into my heart and touched it in such a way that I knew the Lord was present in His Spirit and that impact was tremendous. After that things look so different to me. God uses our heart not the grandeur of words we use. I saw in her eyes hope and a childlike faith.

Many people just do not know the word of God and His promises. Hearing this new truth was such comfort. Comfort knowing the love of the Lord for her.

After a Sunday night service when I had finished preaching and ministering an inmate in jail came up to me and said "one of the ladies that comes to lead bible studies told me to look and see how Jesus gives kisses to you in different ways. Your service kissed me from Jesus". Immediately I heard in my spirit "whatever you do to the least of my brethren you do unto me" Wow, I just kissed Jesus!!!!!! Talk about blessing.

You may not always see or know what impact your words will render, but keep on keeping on. God is blessing all of His people all of the time. I know, you know, that you get the greatest blessing.

God's promises and truths are for all of us, isn't it important to be encouraged, and to encourage one another? Thank you, for in blessing you have blessed.

How will they know if we don't tell them? We all need to be encouraged and to know of God's love. How much He first loved us.

My prayer to you; The Lord richly bless you, that His face always shine on you, that you experience an even greater knowledge of the love God has for you. That you walk in His grace and are assured of that grace and love each day.

That you be in health and prosper in all things as your soul prospers. That you be strengthened with might by His Spirit in the inner man. That Christ may dwell in your heart by faith that you be rooted and grounded in love. That you know the love of Christ, that you may be filled with all the fullness of God, to overflowing, that all grace may abound to you that you may abound to all good works.

All Glory and Honor be to God, who is able to do exceeding abundantly above all we ask or think, through His mighty power at work within us. Amen.

Contents

AN INTERVIEW
WITH JESUS

As I was sitting and praying

Walking out on the back lanai, the morning sun glinting off the pool water, a slight cool breeze brings a hint that fall is near. As I go over to sit at a table, sipping coffee, talking to the Lord, aware of His presence although not physical, notably present, a thought came to me. Have an interview with Jesus.

We have read books, some have even written books, some new, some old books, some are by people who have passed on to be with the Lord, some are still with us. Great men and women of God, Scholars, Pastors, Evangelists, all to read the thoughts of Jesus to get close to the understanding and love of our Glorious God and His full being, The Father, The Son and The Spirit. We study the things people say and have said, commentaries, expositions, what they think or make of something, it is most wonderful and we are inspired by this. But only one person and what He does and has done really makes all the difference in any of our lives. That would be Our Jesus and why He came and what it means to all of us. So why not get the truth straight from the source. Why not interview Jesus?

Jesus is still very much alive! His word is life to all that embrace Him.

Why not Jesus?

He is the Perfect person to Interview. So we will look at some known facts and get into the Interview of:

A Man / God Named Jesus

Purpose

To bring the ungodly to repentance, that they might avert judgment of the non-repented.

To encourage the born again believer to continue in the faith, continue in the overcoming faith of the word of God and the knowledge thereof.

To make clear that while Jesus was on earth He was a man, a man of flesh as you and I, only without sin, He laid down all His Glory and became Man.

> For whatsoever is born of God overcomes the world: and this is the victory that overcomes the world, even our faith. Who is he that overcomes the world, but he that believeth that Jesus is the Son of God. He that believeth on the Son of God hath the witness in himself: he that believeth not God hath made him a liar; because he believeth not the record that God gave

of his Son. And this is the record that God hath given to us eternal life, and this life is in his Son. He that hath the Son hath life; and he that hath not the Son of God hath not life.

1 John 5:4-12 (KJV)

Chapter 1

LOVE AND FAITHFULNESS MEET TOGETHER

In the beginning was the Word, and the Word was with God, and the Word was God. The same was in the beginning with God. All things were made by him; and without him was not anything made that was made. In him was life; and the life was the light of men. And the light shineth in darkness; and the darkness comprehended it not.

John 1:1-5 (KJV)

That preordained all transforming mystery unveiling moment;

The God of all creation, who formed the world and universe, who measured out the waters in the palm hollow of His hand, and meted out heaven with the span, and comprehended the dust of the earth in a measure, and weighed the mountains in scales, and the hills in a balance

Isaiah 40:12 (KJV)

God who is Love looked upon all His creation and Love, Mercy and Truth are met together; righteousness and peace have kissed each other. God, our Glorious God Says, It is time to send My Son,

Mercy and truth are met together; righteousness and peace have kissed each other. Truth shall spring out of the earth; and righteousness shall look down from heaven. Yea, the LORD shall give that which is good; and our land shall yield her increase. Righteousness shall go before him; and shall set us in the way of his steps.

Psalm 85:10-13 (KJV)

The moment when God stepped down from His throne, that glorious magnificent world changing moment, clothed in splendid royal blue, fully prepared for His journey strong and steadfast combining stable and satisfying need for reassurance in a complex world, His glory all about with hosts of heavenly beings surrounding the Throne of The King and Lord of all. The I Am. We catch a glimpse of sapphires and sparkles of precious gems as He is stepping off His throne. Setting all down laying it all aside to become Man, Setting all Glory and Majesty aside to become, The First born Son of God,

Jesus tells us Himself of that story in Matthew 13 "Again, the kingdom of heaven is like unto treasure hid in a field; the which when a man hath found, he hideth, and for joy thereof goeth and selleth all that he hath, and buyeth that field." (Matthew 13:44 KJV)

Mysteries, even the hidden wisdom, which God ordained before the world unto our glory: the mystery of the kingdom of God. According to the revelation of the mystery, this was kept secret since the world began. How He is able to make known unto us the mystery of His will, according to His good pleasure which He hath purposed in Himself. Now to Him that is of power to establish you according to the gospel, and the preaching of Jesus Christ,

And Jesus said unto them, "Unto you it is given to know the mystery of the kingdom of God: but unto them that are without, all these things are done in parables." (Mark 4:11 KJV)

Jesus gives us an example of how to keep our eyes on the joy, on the promise the word of God has given us. That is why it is so very important to know the word and the promises God has made to us. For there is not a moment or situation where we do not need to look to the word for the grace to keep on track, to run our race looking to Jesus in every step we take. He shows us how to keep on track through the power of the Holy Spirit and His word.

> Looking unto Jesus the author and finisher of our faith; who for the joy that was set before him endured the cross, despising the shame, and is set down at the right hand of the throne of God.
>
> Hebrews 12:2 (KJV)

Praise God what a glorious reward.

Jesus says, "Again, the kingdom of heaven is like unto a merchant man, seeking goodly pearls: Who, when he had found one pearl of great price, went and sold all that he had, and bought it. Again, the kingdom of heaven is like unto a net, that was cast into the sea, and gathered of every kind" (Matthew 13:45-47 KJV)

Here Jesus is speaking in parables, His own explanation of the Father's love for mankind. Jesus is telling us of His great love, yet still sinners, how He, God our Father did give His Son and took our sin, sorrow and sickness, so we could have life everlasting. Telling of the secret plan of God from before the world was, The Father, The Word, The Spirit which are one, had for planned.

> For he hath made him to be sin for us, who knew no sin; that we might be made the righteousness of God in him.
>
> 2 Corinthians 5:21 (KJV)

The Christ, The Messiah has laid everything down to come to man's aid. To free man from the captivity and bondages of death and all that its ugliness brings. To restore all that the enemy had taken. We will look even deeper to unfold, explore how, from His own words, Jesus was fully aware of what was to come. Yet, He still stepped down from all glory and splender into this dying, famished, lost world becoming poor so we may be made rich. Knowing, yet still willing to go through the most horrifying death to bring us life.

Jesus was obedient to do the Fathers will, to offer His very best, give of Himself to redeem all mankind.

Jesus goes on to give an even greater explanation of His Fathers love, and why He came to be a Man.

> Which, when it was full, they drew to shore, and sat down, and gathered the good into vessels, but cast the bad away. So shall it be at the end of the world: the angels shall come forth, and sever the wicked from among the just, And shall cast them into the furnace of fire: there shall be wailing and gnashing of teeth. Jesus saith unto them, Have ye understood all these things? They say unto him, Yea, Lord. Then said he unto them, Therefore every scribe which is instructed unto the kingdom of heaven is like unto a man that is an householder, which bringeth forth out of his treasure things new and old.
>
> Matthew 13:48-52 (KJV)

First the field and treasure, then the pearls, then to gather every kind not that any should be lost.

The Jew first, then Gentile, then all mankind to come, there is neither Jew nor Greek, there is neither bond nor free, there is neither male nor female: for ye are all one in Christ Jesus. The Father would that none should perish but all come to repentance.

We see the words, many are called but few are chosen. This indicates you are chosen of God and He has chosen you, but you have your part and that is to choose life.

Jesus said the same thing only in a different parable to the people

He so wants us all to understand. We need to take heed to what the Son says.

> And Jesus answered and spake unto them again by parables, and said, The kingdom of heaven is like unto a certain king, which made a marriage for his son, And sent forth his servants to call them that were bidden to the wedding: and they would not come. Again, he sent forth other servants, saying, Tell them which are bidden, Behold, I have prepared my dinner: my oxen and my fatlings are killed, and all things are ready: come unto the marriage. But they made light of it, and went their ways, one to his farm, another to his merchandise: And the remnant took his servants, and entreated them spitefully, and slew them. But when the king heard thereof, he was wroth: and he sent forth his armies, and destroyed

those murderers, and burned up their city. Then saith he to his servants, The wedding is ready, but they which were bidden were not worthy. Go ye therefore into the highways, and as many as ye shall find, bid to the marriage. So those servants went out into the highways, and gathered together all as many as they found, both bad and good: and the wedding was furnished with guests. And when the king came in to see the guests, he saw there a man which had not on a wedding garment: And he saith unto him, Friend, how camest thou in hither not having a wedding garment? And he was speechless. Then said the king to the servants, Bind him hand and foot, and take him away, and cast him into outer darkness, there shall be weeping and gnashing of teeth. For many are called, but few are chosen.

Matthew 22:1-14 (KJV)

If man would only understand how important you are to The Father. Jesus did not sweeten the pot with false words; He spoke the Truth as to have you understand all is given to you.

In order to receive all He has to offer, you must accept the free gift, believe on Him. Believe on Him also who sent Him. Dress in the garment, put on Jesus and enter in through the door. Jesus is the way, and you cannot enter any other way. Do not be deceived, you cannot work your way into heaven. Only through the Blood of Jesus is man saved. God's Mercy and truth, by grace are you saved, not by anything you can do. It is a free gift.

"For by grace are ye saved through faith; and that not of yourselves: it is the gift of God:" (Ephesians 2:8 KJV)

"Who hath saved us, and called us with an holy calling, not according to our works, but according to his own purpose and grace, which was given us in Christ Jesus before the world began,"(2 Timothy 1:9 KJV)

You know the story of Adam and Eve and how sin came to be on all.

Do you understand sin as it is? Growing up you were told the story of the Garden of Eden, which God made for all of us, then man sinned and we all were kicked out. I heard if only he would have or he could have or even should have, just think of all the things you could have had. Because you cannot go back and change what Adam did, you are left with thoughts of hopelessness. Not knowing all that Jesus did for mankind on the cross and resurrection, left you thinking you missed out on the garden of paradise, giving thoughts loss, and it is just too bad, you can't get it back.

As a young child not knowing all that was done with Adam's sin or understanding all that Jesus did for mankind, I thought, wow, all this because Adam ate fruit and disobeyed God. But I didn't eat that fruit why would a loving God do such a punishment? Who was I to question God? He is a God of judgment? That is the way Satan wants you to think.

Not being told or knowing the truth of what the word tells. You are left thinking "that doesn't seem fair." Let's look at the truth of this, what I was not told as a child.

Wherefore, as by one man, sin entered into the world, death by sin; and so death passed upon all men, for that all have sinned: that one man's sin was so very much more; it transferred all in to the hands of death. The lie or lack of knowledge of the truth was to trick us into not understanding the depths that one choice brought, to blame God for over re-acting, or Adam was ignorant, to somehow make light of it, and to hide the true fact, that sin brought with it; Death to every living creature and plant, the curse was then on us all. Not just a sin, all Adam's seed would have the curse of sin and death on them. That one choice turned all mankind over to the father of death and decay.

Glory to God, until I had my own encounter, my own revelation of Jesus and the promises, the truth of the free gift, the better covenant I have through Christ. Glory that is something to shout about!

No my friend, Life in Christ is so very much more than just a grazing place.

When sin came upon man it brought all sickness, poverty in every area of our being, sorrow, torment, disease, grief, transgressions, iniquities and the chastisement needed for our peace. Sin took it; sin brought shame guilt and remorse and took our reassurance of God's love, peace and glory, and left lies, bondage and captivity to death in every area of our being. Not only the ground we walk on but our body, spirit, soul, mind all that we see and the unseen. Sin is not glamorous in any way or trivial to be taken lightly. Sin, the ugly truth, destroys lives, brings death, and decay filled with all matter of trepidation. When it rears its ugly head, it is never "good". The dyeing decaying of us all is a very ugly picture.

Despair not you who are in Christ, have life. You have life in every area of your being. All that the enemy took, Christ and His Anointing took back, out of the hand of Satan and his workers.

In reading Isaiah 53 you see the Word of God says just what Jesus was to do and HE DID!

Glory to God!

> Who hath believed our report? and to whom is the arm of the Lord revealed? For he shall grow up before him as a tender plant, and as a root out of a dry ground: he hath no form or comeliness; and when we shall see him, there is no beauty that we should desire him. He is despised and rejected of men; a man of sorrows, and acquainted with grief: and we hid as it were our faces from him; he was despised, and we esteemed him not. Surely he hath borne our grief's, and carried our sorrows: yet we did esteem him stricken, smitten of God, and afflicted. But he was wounded for our transgressions, he was bruised for our iniquities: the chastisement of our peace was upon him; and with his stripes we are healed. All we

like sheep have gone astray; we have turned every one to his own way; and the Lord hath laid on him the iniquity of us all. He was oppressed, and he was afflicted, yet he opened not his mouth: he is brought as a lamb to the slaughter, and as a sheep before her shearers is dumb, so he openeth not his mouth. He was taken from prison and from judgment: and who shall declare his generation? for he was cut off out of the land of the living: for the transgression of my people was he stricken. And he made his grave with the wicked, and with the rich in his death; because he had done no violence, neither was any deceit in his mouth. Yet it pleased the Lord to bruise him; he hath put him to grief: when thou shalt make his soul an offering for sin, he shall see his seed, he shall prolong his days, and the pleasure of the Lord shall prosper in his hand. He shall see of the travail of his soul, and shall be satisfied: by his knowledge shall my righteous servant justify many; for he shall bear their iniquities. Therefore will I divide him a portion with the great, and he shall divide the spoil with the strong; because he hath poured out his soul unto death: and he was numbered with the transgressors; and he bare the sin of many, and made intercession for the transgressors.

Isaiah 53:1-12 (KJV)

The word of God, Jesus, my friend, knew all this, He is the Word made man. He was so fully aware of what was to come. In the Garden of Gethsemane Jesus prayed to the Father asking if this could pass from Him. But this was not news to Jesus, He already knew what was to come. This is why Jesus came, Jesus was fully aware from before creation.

Thank you My Lord Jesus! Thank You.

> But now is Christ raisin from the dead, and become the first fruits of them that slept. For since by man came death, by man came also the resurrection of the dead. For as in Adam all die, even so in Christ shall all be made alive. But every man in his own order: Christ the first fruits; afterward they that are Christ's at his coming. Then cometh the end, when he shall have delivered up the kingdom to God, even the Father; when he shall have put down all rule and all authority and power. For he must reign, till he hath put all enemies under his feet. The last enemy that shall be destroyed is death.
>
> 1 Corinthians 15:20-26 (KJV)

Jesus, fully aware of every jot, every tittle, every word, and every sin death brings. Aware of every person, past, present and to ever be born. Jesus, my friend, knew what He was stepping into way before He took that first step off His Throne, for all of mankind. He always was, He is the first and the last, the beginning and the end, the alpha and omega, together with the Father, the Word (the Son), and the Spirit

Why?

Jesus did it all, for God who is Love, that we who are in Jesus, in Christ, have life everlasting.

Victory is yours, who are in Christ, to all who come to Him, Believe and Confess Him as Lord.

Jesus forewarns us over and over with His words." The thief cometh not, but for to steal, and to kill, and to destroy: I am come that they might have life, and that they might have it more abundantly." (John 10:10 KJV)

> Beware lest any man spoil you through philosophy and vain deceit, after the tradition of men, after the rudiments of the world, and not after Christ. For in him dwelleth all the fulness of the Godhead bodily. And ye are complete in him, which is the head of all principality and power: In whom also ye are circumcised with the circumcision made without hands, in putting off the body of the sins of the flesh by the circumcision of Christ: Buried with him in baptism, wherein also ye are risen with him through the faith of the operation of God, who hath raised him from the dead. And you, being dead in your sins and the uncircumcision of your flesh, hath he quickened together with him, having forgiven you all trespasses; Blotting out the handwriting of ordinances that was against us, which was contrary to us, and took it out of the way, nailing it to his cross; And having spoiled principalities and powers, he made a shew of them openly, triumphing over them in it.
>
> Colossians 2:8-15 (KJV)

Glory Be!! Glory be to God!!!

Choose this day who you will serve, as for me and my house I serve the Lord.

Are you washed in the Blood, are you white as snow? Do you Believe and Confess Him as Lord? Are you the righteousness of God, in Him?

Or are you blinded? Are you Unknowledgeable?

> In whom the god of this world hath blinded the minds of them which believe not, lest the light of the glorious gospel of Christ, who is the image of God, should shine unto them.
>
> 2 Corinthians 4:4 (KJV)

There will come a day my friend very soon that My Jesus we shall see!

And every knee will bow and every tongue will confess Jesus is Lord.

Jesus gives you "The invitation".

Turn to page 173.

Take a moment and we will pray.

Chapter 2

THE BIRTH

And it came to pass in those days, that there went out a decree from Caesar Augustus that all the world should be taxed. (And this taxing was first made when Cyrenius was governor of Syria.) And all went to be taxed, every one into his own city. And Joseph also went up from Galilee, out of the city of Nazareth, into Judaea, unto the city of David, which is called Bethlehem; (because he was of the house and lineage of David:) To be taxed with Mary his espoused wife, being great with child. And so it was, that, while they were there, the days were accomplished that she should be delivered. And she brought forth her firstborn son, and wrapped him in swaddling clothes, and laid him in a manger; because there was no room for them in the inn. And there were in the same country shepherds abiding in the field, keeping watch over their flock by night.

And, lo, the angel of the Lord came upon them, and the glory of the Lord shone round about them: and they were sore afraid. And the angel said unto them, Fear not: for, behold, I bring you good tidings of great joy, which shall be to all people. For unto you is born this day in the city of David a Savior, which is Christ the Lord. And this shall be a sign unto you; Ye shall find the babe wrapped in swaddling clothes, lying in a manger. And suddenly there was with the angel a multitude of the heavenly host praising God, and saying, Glory to God in the highest, and on earth peace, good will toward men. And it came to pass, as the angels were gone away from them into heaven, the shepherds said one to another, Let us now go even unto Bethlehem, and see this thing which is come to pass, which the Lord hath made known unto us.

Luke 2:1-15 (KJV)

And the angel said unto them, Fear not: for behold I bring you good tidings of great joy, which shall be to all people.

Fear not I bring you good tidings and great joy! Then suddenly! Can you see?

The heavens are full of the glory of the Lord! Multitudes of heavenly host praising and singing honor to the glory of God in the highest and on earth peace, good will to man.

That is a love song of the highest magnitude. The Kiss of love where mercy and truth are met together, a Savior is born this day. Glory to God!!

And the shepherds said one to another, Let us now go even unto Bethlehem, and see this thing which is come to pass, which the Lord hath made known unto us. They went to behold the child.

The child who came for all mankind, for the common to the elite, He came for us all. From shepherds to kings, you see we are all the same, lost in sin and need our Savior.

The adoration of the arrival of the King and Lord Jesus was a proclamation for worshiping the infant Messiah, the child Jesus, The King of Kings and Lord of Lords.

Glory is to God, the presentation of the wise men and the entourage that followed, ready to attend with gifts for The King. Be of highest magnitude of praise and honor. Bearing gifts for the child, the Son of God, with gold, frankincense and myrrh to present to the mighty King of Kings. As the wise men entered the house, overtaken with joy that filled each one of their hearts, as they behold the child with His mother, what joy unspeakable filled the room bowing down worshipping Him. Blessing and honor and glory and power be unto Him.

I can only imagine the magnitude of wonderful gifts of fine spender being brought as the custom of the time, a caravan of spender bearing gifts.

Three wise men traveling far, led by the truth, the Spirit, and by the light of The Star.

On the eighth day the child was circumcised, His name was called Jesus, Which was so named of the angel before He was conceived in the womb.

Praise and honor to the abundant LOVE that came down from above.

Mary purified

On the day of her purification according to Law of Moses, they brought Him to Jerusalem, to present Him to the Lord; as it is written in the law of the Lord, Every male that opens the womb shall be called holy to the Lord. And to offer a sacrifice according to that which is said in the law of the Lord,

Mary and Joseph went to Jerusalem to the temple to present the child to the Lord. She offered a pair of turtledoves, or two young pigeons.

In Leviticus 12: 2-8 says a lamb of the first year for a burnt offering and a young pigeon or turtledove for a sin offering, going on to say if you did not bring a lamb then she brings two turtles, or two young pigeon.

It has been written and thought by some that she could not afford to offer a lamb so she brought a pair of turtledoves, or two young pigeons. What are they thinking? What does the Spirit say? Realizing in my spirit, The Lord said when you read My word, read it in LOVE, all that the

Father is, is love. His entire life Jesus spoke the way for us to see His Father. Do we not see, the Lamb was in her arms! She would not bring two lambs, only one is worthy; looking at the things of God through His eyes, eyes of love, not our own reason or flesh. When we read the word through the love of God by the Spirit, the Word speaks so clearly. Simeon, took Jesus up in his arms and Blessed God and said,

> Lord, now lettest thou thy servant depart in peace, according to thy word: For mine eyes have seen thy salvation, Which thou hast prepared before the face of all people; A light to lighten the Gentiles, and the glory of thy people Israel. And Joseph and his mother marveled at those things which were spoken of him. And Simeon blessed them, and said unto Mary his mother, Behold, this child is set for the fall and rising again of many in Israel; and for a sign which shall be spoken against; (Yea, a sword shall pierce through thy own soul also,) that the thoughts of many hearts may be revealed.

> Luke 2:29-35 (KJV)

Anna a prophetess served God with fasting and prayers night and day. Coming in that instant gave thanks and adoration unto the Lord, spoke of Him to all that looked for redemption in Jerusalem

Behold the Lamb of God who takes away the sins of the world.

But with the precious blood of Christ, as of a lamb without blemish and without spot: Who verily was foreordained before the foundation of the world, but was manifest in these last times for you, Who by him do believe in God, that raised him up from the dead, and gave him glory; that your faith and hope might be in God.

1 Peter 1:19-21 (KJV)

Glory to God!!! Amen Peter Amen!!

The child grew, and waxed strong in spirit, filled with wisdom: and the grace of God was upon Him. ....

We find Jesus at age 12 in the temple sitting in the midst of the doctors, both hearing them, and asking them questions. The Mishna of the first-century Jewish practice, religious instruction would have become more intense for Jesus upon his reaching twelve. I read that the custom of bar mitzvah for a thirteen-year-old Jewish boy was not in place at this time.

Jesus at age twelve was growing in knowledge and wisdom and His identity. Closeness to His Father was important, strength and power in spirit, also was increased, a hunger for the presence of the Father and truth a comfort to His spirit. Yet Jesus' discussion with the officials leaves those who listen amazed at his understanding and his answers. At the tender age of twelve, Jesus already shows signs of possessing great wisdom.

Mary and Joseph spent three days looking for Jesus. When they left to return home, thinking that He was with them when they started their journey to their own city. To find out that the boy was not with them, they went back to look for Him. When finding, His mother asked, Son why have you thus dealt with us, and he said unto them, how is it that ye sought me? Would you not know that I must be in my Father's house?

The very same is for us, we shall always know how to find Him, all we have to do is reach out to Him. Take time to call on His Name. He is waiting to hear from you.

Jesus shows us it is the sprit that prospers not the flesh. Knowing who we are in Christ is the key to us living a life of victory or defeat. For He has made Him to be sin for us, who knew no sin; that we might be made the righteousness of God in Him. It is so crucial that you know who you are in Christ. And to know all that you have been given through His blood. Not only today's forgiveness we have our past, our present, and all future sin under the blood, if you sin you can have that same washing; You must keep our eyes on who you are in Christ, on the new birth your mind renewed with the washing of the word.

> Therefore if any man be in Christ, he is a new creature: old things are passed away; behold, all things are become new. And all things are of God, who hath reconciled us to himself by Jesus Christ, and hath given to us the ministry of reconciliation;

To wit, that God was in Christ, reconciling the world unto himself, not imputing their trespasses unto them; and hath committed unto us the word of reconciliation.

2 Corinthians 5:17-19 (KJV)

Glory to God!!!!
My friends get this truth deep in your heart.

Christ hath redeemed us from the curse of the law, being made a curse for us: for it is written, Cursed is every one that hangeth on a tree: That the blessing of Abraham might come on the Gentiles through Jesus Christ; that we might receive the promise of the Spirit through faith.

Galatians 3:13-14 (KJV)

For as many of you as have been baptized into Christ have put on Christ. There is neither Jew nor Greek, there is neither bond nor free, there is neither male nor female: for ye are all one in Christ Jesus. And if ye be Christ's, then are ye Abraham's seed, and heirs according to the promise.

Galatians 3:27-29 (KJV)

You that are in Christ are the seed of Abraham, and the very coolest and most awesome part is, you can trace the seed all the way to God our Father. How cool is that!!!!

And the Holy Ghost descended in a bodily shape like a dove upon him, and a voice came from heaven, which said, Thou art my beloved Son; in thee I am well pleased. And Jesus himself began to be about thirty years of age, being (as was supposed) the son of Joseph, which was the son of Heli, Which was the son of Matthat, which was the son of Levi, which was the son of Melchi, which was the son of Janna, which was the son of Joseph, Which was the son of Mattathias, which was the son of Amos, which was the son of Naum, which was the son of Esli, which was the son of Nagge, Which was the son of Maath, which was the son of Mattathias, which was the son of Semei, which was the son of Joseph, which was the son of Juda, Which was the son of Joanna, which was the son of Rhesa, which was the son of Zorobabel, which was the son of Salathiel, which was the son of Neri, Which was the son of Melchi, which was the son of Addi, which was the son of Cosam, which was the son of Elmodam, which was the son of Er, Which was the son of Jose, which was the son of Eliezer, which was the son of Jorim, which was the son of Matthat, which was the son of Levi, Which was the son of Simeon, which was the son of Juda, which was the son of Joseph, which was the son of Jonan, which was the son of Eliakim, Which was the son of Melea, which was the son of Menan, which was the son of Mattatha, which was the son of Nathan, which was the son of David, Which was the son of Jesse, which was the son of Obed, which was the son of Booz, which was the son of Salmon, which was the son of Naasson, Which was the son of Aminadab, which was the son of Aram, which was the son of Esrom, which was the son of Phares, which was the son of Juda, Which was the son of Jacob, which was the son of Isaac, which was the son of Abraham, which was the son of Thara, which was the son of Nachor, Which was the son of Saruch, which was the son of Ragau, which was the son of Phalec, which was the son of Heber, which was the son of Sala, Which was the son of Cainan, which was the son of Arphaxad, which was the son of Sem, which was the son of Noe, which was the son of Lamech, Which was the son of Mathusala, which was the son of Enoch, which was the son of Jared, which was the son of Maleleel, which was the son of Cainan, Which was the son of Enos, which was the son of Seth, which was the son of Adam, which was the son of God.

Luke 3:22-38 (KJV)

In Christ you are the seed of God you are God's child. Glory to GOD!!!!!!! WOW Think on that……

"Ye are of God, little children, and have overcome them: because greater is he that is in you, than he that is in the world." (1John 4:4 KJV)

You are of God; you are the Righteousness of God in Him in Christ. You are free! There is no condemnation in Christ Jesus. You are reconciled to God. Only the enemy and our thoughts accuse and remember sin. To God it is simply not there. It was placed on the cross. Do not keep it.

Jesus took it and He "Blotting out the handwriting of ordinances that was against us, which was contrary to us, and took it out of the way, nailing it to his cross; And having spoiled principalities and powers, he made a shew of them openly, triumphing over them in it." (Colossians 2:14-15 KJV)

Ask for forgiveness if you have sinned. Forgive others, and yourself. When any thought or remembrance of sin or occurrence of sin shows up, put it on the cross, and leave it with Jesus's blood.

Jesus told us who to look to for everything,

What are you thinking? Be not deceived the devil does not want you in Christ. So every lie, trick or way he can keep you blinded, he will. Rich or poor, big or small, happy or sad, good or bad, healthy or sick, we all need what only Jesus The Savior can provide. You do not have to be so broken or falling apart to come to Jesus.

Even if you think you have it all and things are just "fine". You are being deceived, for without Christ, you have nothing. You may miss your only chance at Life," the New Birth," which only Jesus gives. Our war is not the people we see each day or the place we work, or the place we live or our family or neighbors, as trying as times may be. Our war is all unseen by man's eye.

> For though we walk in the flesh, we do not war after the flesh: (For the weapons of our warfare are not carnal, but mighty through God to the pulling

down of strong holds;) Casting down imaginations, and every high thing that exalteth itself against the knowledge of God, and bringing into captivity every thought to the obedience of Christ;

2 Corinthians 10:3-5 (KJV)

I call heaven and earth to record this day against you, that I have set before you life and death, blessing and cursing: therefore choose life, that both thou and thy seed may live: That thou mayest love the Lord thy God, and that thou mayest obey his voice, and that thou mayest cleave unto him: for he is thy life, and the length of thy days: that thou mayest dwell in the land which the Lord sware unto thy fathers, to Abraham, to Isaac, and to Jacob, to give them.

Deuteronomy 30:19-20 (KJV)

You first have to choose. Choosing the Blessing chooses to bring Jesus in your heart. To repent making Him Lord of our life, to believe in God. Then you have to know what the Spirit tells you, by reading the word of God. Seeing what God has promised for His Children His family and His Kingdom.

Jesus gives you "The invitation".

Turn to page 173.

Take a moment and we will pray.

And the child became a Man.

Chapter 3

QUESTION ONE

Questions I asked myself, questions, what in this interview does Jesus most want us to know?

I would suppose that would be my first question, in that I have a thousand directions to take, but what would benefit the reader the most? Who would read this? My heart full of love and trust in Him would ask a different question than a lost soul. So in praying and seeking direction I went on-line and asked a question, what would you want to ask Jesus? The search pulled up questions people have put out on line. To my heart's dismay I read questions that were mostly filled with torment and pain. They ranged from thinking of oneself so unworthy to being vulgar and quite satanic. At first I was taken back to say the least and all kind of thoughts came to mind. How could they say that, and where would I start, and this just breaks the heart.......

Then I stopped, looked to Jesus and His word, seeing it so clearly, of course, the Lord is so loving, forgiving and faithful and His Mercies are new every day, this is not news to God, Jesus knew all of this before He ever came down and became man. As Jesus walked, as man during His earthly ministry, Jesus always shows compassion on the people and He healed them all, He was filled with compassion. Just think about it for a moment, the people from all over surrounding cities, thousands of people with all kinds of diseases, afflictions, possessed of spirits you name it and they had it, yet they all still came to see Jesus. Never did He shun a person that is why He came, to free you from all the lies and sin. Jesus had compassion not sympathy, He didn't feel sorry for the people or overwhelmed, Jesus was moved to do something, to pray and to heal.

Jesus shows us what to do. To pray, to have compassion on each person, pray for the people who asked all the questions. Pray for healing and salvation. Not judge in any way good and bad or feel sorry for anyone but to be moved with compassion and do something, intercede for them pray in faith for their salvation, to open the eyes and hearts to bring truth in, the truth that sets you free, free from all sin and death keeps us from. Believe God for it, then thank God and believe it is done and from time to time when the Lord places them on your heart, give thanksgiving and praise to the Lord on their behalf.

Not only the lost struggle with the tricks that Satan and his workers try, but, Christians also struggle. Satan not only tries to get you to sin but to keep the truth from you, so that you don't and are not able to walk in all the life giving promises of God, to know the love from God in His word that is yours in Christ through faith and the power of the Holy Spirit. To keep the truth from you, the truth that he has been defeated and that, in every area of your life, Jesus has victory over, it is a done deal. You are complete in Christ and have VICTORY.

Believing that Jesus's words are to everyone, to increase their overcoming strength in Him and to continually encourage lead guide and provide. Bring salvation and hope for the future. Show all how to live a victorious life by following His example, His word, by the in lighting and washing of the Holy Spirit. That you could never come up against anything, that the word of God hasn't already taken care of. By following and looking at everything Jesus did and said you will always find a way. Jesus never lost sight of His purpose, of His calling, no matter what came at Him He kept His eye on the Father, as we are to study and keep our focus on Him.

Jesus says:

> therefore take no thought, saying, What shall we eat? or, What shall we drink? or, Wherewithal shall we be clothed? (For after all these things do the Gentiles seek:) for your heavenly Father knoweth that ye have need of all these things. But seek ye first the kingdom of God, and his righteousness; and all these things shall be added unto you. Take therefore

no thought for the morrow: for the morrow shall take thought for the things of itself. Sufficient unto the day is the evil thereof.

Matthew 6:31-34 (KJV)

Let's take a closer look at what He is saying in Matthew 6; Jesus is giving instruction on several issues, but let's look at the verses 25 – 34.

Therefore I say unto you, Take no thought for your life, what ye shall eat, or what ye shall drink; nor yet for your body, what ye shall put on. Is not the life more than meat, and the body than raiment? Behold the fowls of the air: for they sow not, neither do they reap, nor gather into barns; yet your heavenly Father feedeth them. Are ye not much better than they? Which of you by taking thought can add one cubit unto his stature? And why take ye thought for raiment? Consider the lilies of the field, how they grow; they toil not, neither do they spin: And yet I say unto you, That even Solomon in all his glory was not arrayed like one of these. Wherefore, if God so clothe the grass of the field, which today is, and tomorrow is cast into the oven, shall he not much more clothe you, O ye of little faith? Therefore take no thought, saying, What shall we eat? or, What shall we drink? or, Wherewithal shall we be clothed? (For after all these things do the Gentiles seek:) for your heavenly Father knoweth that ye have need of all these things. But seek ye first the kingdom of God, and his righteousness; and all these things shall be added unto you. Take therefore no thought for the morrow: for the morrow shall take thought for the things of itself. Sufficient unto the day is the evil thereof.

Matthew 6:25-34 (KJV)

Making decisions based on lies placed in your own heart renders unintended fruit, not being based on the truth of what God says. Decisions based on lies, even with the best of intentions do not produce the intended fruit. That causes not only you, but the people you hold most dear in your life, pain. Thus you, doing the best you could with the knowledge or tools you had at the time, this also goes for your parents and people you may have dealings with, returned very undesired fruit as well. When you have an understanding of where this undesirable fruit comes from, by the understanding and truth of the word of God, you can surrender forgiveness, forgiveness to others, and to yourself. Not carrying shame or blame that the enemy wants you to carry in your heart. In my own walk with Jesus, that is one of the first scriptures I was given to learn some years ago, and I am still learning from it. Through it all, not that my race is over, in fact I am trusting the Lord for a well, peaceful, long life, so I have a ways to go, Jesus has never ever let me down or left me. He is always with me, always forgiving, always loving and His mercy is always new every day.

Being a child of God does not mean you will not ever sin or believe a lie from hell. It means as a child of God you have an advocate with the Father and when you ask for forgiveness He is faithful and just to forgive. That does not in any way give any one a right to sin, only a way out should you stumble. You can mess up by acting out the lies that Satan tells, acting on a thought that has shame or blame in it, then that choice is founded on a lie, not what the word of God says. That is why it is so very important to know and hold on to the word of God. You never stop learning or growing in Christ as long as you keep on Seeking first the kingdom of God, and His righteousness, doing this above all, diligently go after God, desire to know more of Him. If you make a mistake, ask for God's forgiveness, know it is forgiven, and know it is on the cross.

The word of God covers everything you will ever encounter on this earth. Worry, anxiety and concern, whatever, you name it, whatever you face, be it a thousand times a day, for as long as you have breath, whatever you face, the word of God has overcoming power. If you have children and grandchildren the situations may be tripled, but the word of God always has a way to overcome any and all situations. Glory!!!!

This is not to say don't plan or be prepared, but to plan and be prepared in all things seeking first God and His righteousness. His creature, God's way of doing something, whatever is right or just in itself, whatever conforms to the revealed will of God.

When you are seeking God first, as a believer, you cannot afford to be slack but you have to choose to side with God's word continually. It's not something you do once. It's a process of choosing to believe and act upon the word of God over and over, in every circumstance. We have to press in on the word of God every day. Take time, make time, even if it cost you some sleep it is by far a much better price to pay than if the evil one gets a hold of things.

You are not able to run a marathon if you have not had proper preparation or have the right nourishment, your body will not stand up, you would not have energy in reserve or the stamina to continue. That is the same in regards to spending time with God and your bible,

Then and only then will your house be built on the rock, you have built it with the Love of God and our faith in Him.

When a storm comes you are ready, your house is strong your foundation is intact, nothing will move it. Living in Florida you know to be ready and what is needed, to be prepared. You are familiar with what is needed to be safe. You know how to prepare before a hurricane comes so you are able to withstand, should power go out you have food to sustain you through the rough times.

When the storm hits land is not the time to start building a home, nor is it the time to start boarding up your home. You had best be prepared before it starts to even come close.

That is the same with the word of God and the knowledge of God's word, when the enemy comes at you, you will need to pull from your source of strength, the strength that is deep in your heart, that is so strong in you that when a situation comes up, and you open your mouth, it is God's word that comes out and you find the Anointed Power and Strength that will with stand any force.

To know God, and to know His righteousness; we find the word righteousness used here in Matthew. –In the Strong's Concordance, " Dikahyosoonay, is the character or act quality of being right or just;" (Strong's Concordance) You may explain it as to denote an attribute of God, Gods righteousness, all that He is, Gods character of being, what is right and just revealed will of God.

To come to know God's character, the "knowing" of God, and His, Righteousness. Smith Wigglesworth talks of the KNOWING. When you know a person or are fully persuaded, the phrase, you have heard "I know that I know" and nothing will change that. The knowing for yourself because God has done something for you and nothing could change that fact. The knowing of a person and his character only comes from spending time with that person.

Jesus said "But go ye and learn what that meaneth, I will have mercy, and not sacrifice: for I am not come to call the righteous, but sinners to repentance." (Matthew 9:13 KJV)

God is a God of love, Jesus made reference to this statement when He was asked about the Sabbath, "But if ye had known what this meaneth, I will have mercy, and not sacrifice, ye would not have condemned the guiltless." (Matthew 12:7 KJV) The" knowing" by experience. To be able to experience for yourself, know for yourself, through the knowing, He did it for you and it is a truth, a reality. God is a God of love not punishment, a God of mercy, not sacrifice, and every one or thing that concerns you, He is more than able, for Jesus said "But I say unto you, That in this place is one greater than the temple." (Matthew 12:6 KJV) Experiencing and knowing. They were more concerned about following the rules of the Sabbath, than the Love of the Sabbath. You hear people say you never know someone till you live with them; well that is just what you have to do. Jesus says,

> Abide in me, and I in you. As the branch cannot bear fruit of itself, except it abide in the vine; no more can ye, except ye abide in me. I am the vine, ye are the branches: He that abideth in me, and I in him, the same bringeth forth much fruit: for without me ye can do nothing. If ye abide in me, and my words abide in you, ye shall ask what ye will, and it shall be done unto you. Herein is my Father glorified, that ye bear much fruit; so shall ye be my disciples. As the Father hath loved me, so have I loved you: continue ye in my love.
>
> John 15:4-9 (KJV)

Using this illustration; you are an adamant football fan, you have this great team, you travel all over to watch them play, and player number 88 is the main reason. You study all his moves, over and over, you almost know what he is going to do before he even makes the play, and you've got it down. Oh what you would give to meet number 88 the player, to shake his hand wow even be so bold as to talk to him. The game is over your team won and number 88 was outstanding, you are out in the parking lot walking to your car, a quite large fellow walks right by you, you look right at him and pass him by. Only to find out after, that, that was your number 88!!! Oh what dismay, he was in street clothes, you didn't know, oh if only you would have known, what you would have said to him.

How well do you know Jesus? Do you look for Him in others? Do you see Him in yourself? Are you always able to spot Him? Can you pick Him out in a crowd?

The priests of the Old Testament had daily offerings along with special feasts celebrations, the people daily had tasks unto the Lord, why? God was before them every morning every day.

> They kept also the feast of tabernacles, as it is written, and offered the daily burnt offerings by number, according to the custom, as the duty of every day required;
>
> Ezra 3:4 (KJV)

When you come to worship and praise, when you give of yourself to God, give Him your day and all it holds. Through the Blood of Jesus you are new every day, your offering and gift to God has been paid and the Blood given on our behalf so you can come boldly in to the throne of God. He gives us grace and mercy in time of need. Is there a day you do not need God? In Romans, we are urged, therefore brothers, in view of God's mercy, to offer of yourself as living sacrifices, holy and pleasing to God. This is your spiritual act of worship. Giving of yourself to God each day in Worship to Him, reminds you who you belong to. Your debt has been paid in full. It prepares you for your daily tasks, that you do all things in Christ, for apart from Him you can do nothing.

Spending time with God, what a wonderful way to start and end your day, for you never leave His presence, Nor He ours. God says in His word "I will never leave you or for sake you."

In Hebrews it says; "Let your conversation be without covetousness; and be content with such things as ye have: for he hath said, I will never leave thee, nor forsake thee. So that we may boldly say, The Lord is my helper, and I will not fear what man shall do unto me." (Hebrews 13:5 KJV)

> but the fruit of the Spirit is love, joy, peace, patience, gentleness, goodness, faith, Meekness, temperance: against such there is no law. And they that are Christ's have crucified the flesh with the affections

and lusts. If we live in the Spirit, let us also walk in the Spirit.

Galatians 5:22-25 (KJV)

Not the way of the flesh but His Spirit not your fruit but His fruit.

Jesus says:

> And Jesus came and spoke unto them, saying, All power is given unto me in heaven and in earth. Go ye therefore, and teach all nations, baptizing them in the name of the Father, and of the Son, and of the Holy Ghost: Teaching them to observe all things whatsoever I have commanded you: and, lo, I am with you always, even unto the end of the world. Amen.

Matt 28:18-20 (KJV)

Jesus also told of the comforter He will send. "Nevertheless I tell you the truth; it is expedient for you that I go away: for if I go not away, the Comforter will not come unto you; but if I depart, I will send him unto you." (John 16:7 KJV) He went on to say "And, behold, I send the promise of my Father upon you: but tarry ye in the city of Jerusalem, until ye be endued with power from on high. (Luke 24:49 KJV)

God in His word has promised us "He will never leave us", Jesus said "He is with us always even unto the end of time" and you have "the promise of my Father upon you" the Comforter and Power from on high. You have all you need and MORE. You can walk in power from on high and the "Knowing" the Blessed Trinity, God the Father, Jesus the Son, and The Holy Spirit.

Or walk in our flesh

As Jesus forewarns us in Matthew, "No man can serve two masters: for either he will hate the one, and love the other; or else he will hold to the one, and despise the other. Ye cannot serve God and mammon. (Matthew 6:24 KJV) or as Jesus said God Knows you have need of all these things." But seek ye first the kingdom of God, and his righteousness; and all these things shall be added unto you." (Matthew 6:32-33 KJV)

When you start to experience an increase in the knowledge of just how much God loves you and His Power in that Love, you will experience an increase in the knowledge of who you are in Christ. Thank You Jesus! Thank You Father God! Thank You Holy Spirit!

Chapter 4

TESTIMONY

My intention was to get into the walk of Jesus leading up to the cross. But the Spirit has a different direction so I will be obedient and follow His promptings and share a part of my walk.

While I was writing this, I had come to a point in my own life I needed to set this aside as I faced an additional tremendous challenge. I needed help NOW from my Jesus, my God. How do I do this how do I overcome this Lord? I am standing on your word for so very many situations now, why such a fight?

In September of 2012 we moved my mother in with us from a nursing home, she had come to the point that she was unable to really do anything for herself; she was given the diagnoses of having Alzheimer's and the last few months of her life, left. She was unable to even walk a foot or stand.

In October my daughter found a huge mass in her, talk about needing to look beyond the situation and what you see, and walk in faith. I had to stop writing and start reaching to my source of help.

So I went to the word of God and dove in heart first, I know what He has done for me in the past and the healing that He has done. I know the healing He has done for my children and for myself, we are talking miracles, but why was this so hard why did it seem like such a big fight? Why was it such a battle? We prayed for my daughter I laid hands on her and prayed.

Reading in the word of how Jesus healed them all and when any sign of doubt would arise I would look to Jesus and in my mind visualize Him praying for her. In all of the healings Jesus did, He didn't ever say you must do this or that first, Jesus never put conditions on healing. He healed them all. It is up to you after the healing, you read of Him saying after the healing was manifested to go in peace and sin no more. But Jesus healed them all. Every time a fear thought would come up I would picture in my mind Jesus looking at the father of the young girl and saying "only believe" and I would say yes Lord I believe.

I recall when saying to someone "I know it is not cancer," and them saying "we don't know that," I replied, "I know it is not." Then I thought well aren't you going to look stupid if this is. I quickly cut that thought off, and remembered seeing Jesus saying "only believe"

I asked The Holy Spirit to help me, help me understand what I needed to do, I read the Scriptures on what we have in the Name of Jesus, and what the believer has in Christ as to His Authority. I researched all the things that the Cross covered, all that Jesus went through for us. I had prayed for my mother and I am trusting God in this situation. I asked myself was the sickness that plagued my mother able to bring doubt in my heart? Was seeing this every day bringing doubt? I recalled when she was in the nursing home and I would see all the people so very sick and the ugliness of all the hurt caused by the enemy and how he is such a destroyer, a killer. The people that were in the same cottage as mom were so sweet and so easy to minister to. We would sing songs of praise, bringing communion in to them on Sundays. Family members that happened to be there would also receive. Never the less to see the bodies of these lovely people from week to week, deteriorating and my mother being one of them, is not an easy sight to look at. One thing for sure, I had to submerge in to teaching and the word of God just to keep afloat.

Remembering also when told that one of my other daughters was diagnosed with MS I refused to believe it. I would not give fear nor that word a place in my heart, and I am still standing on the promises God gave me for her. Five years have passed and I am still praising God for her healing. She had a MRI done a few months passed on her head and spine and the lesion that was there is gone! Praise

Jesus!!! You may ask, is she 100 present healed? I know the answer is yes. I believe she is, to the Glory of God.

The Holy Spirit placed in my heart don't look at the torment of what is going on with your mother, look to the love of God for your help. It came down to this one thing, God's Love and Faith in His Love.

What I was seeing was all that the enemy took and how he left my mother. I was walking by sight and without realizing it, I was looking at the problem not the solution. Even if it was not the same problem, it was no solution for anyone. Seeing her that way was enough to bring in doubt pulling me down. The Holy Spirit placed in my heart to show her Gods Love; look on her with His love, and think on good things.

> Be careful for nothing; but in everything by prayer and supplication with thanksgiving let your requests be made known unto God. And the peace of God, which passeth all understanding, shall keep your hearts and minds through Christ Jesus. Finally, brethren, whatsoever things are true, whatsoever things are honest, whatsoever things are just, whatsoever things are pure, whatsoever things are lovely, whatsoever things are of good report; if there be any virtue, and if there be any praise, think on these things.
>
> Philippians 4:6-8 (KJV)

I could not let doubt have a place no matter what thoughts tried to enter my mind or what anyone would say. I could not let doubt, fear, or the lies from hell to become my thoughts. So when I would dress mom and change her and clean and feed her, I would play and sing praise songs to the Lord. I ordered CD's from KCM that are full of praise and worship with the word of God that really lifts up your thoughts to God. I play them for mom when she goes to sleep. The Lord placed on my heart to purchase a gift for my mother, a ring and a watch (a little bling). So each day when I place the ring on her finger, I would tell her, "this ring is to tell you, that Jesus loves you," and when I put her watch on her, I would tell her, "no matter what ever the time is, day or night God is always with you He never leaves you." I also keep the word of God on CD's going 24x7 in our home. I held on to my faith, entering in the Holy of Holy and finding grace and mercy in my time of need.

Being encouraged by words from songs that build you up, To Him who sits on the throne and unto the Lamb; Be Blessing and Glory and Honor and Power Forever! What tremendous love of our Father, love that carried me up and over….. Singing songs of praise and worship, praising God over every nonproductive thought that came in I would either start to praise God all the more or I would pray in the Spirit. But I will not faint.

Still the fight seemed to go on. Still it just was not settled. God always settles things in my heart and I have peace in that matter, something to hold on to.

Then the day came, I was to meet my daughter at the Doctor's office, we were to go to get the results of the biopsy.

I could not tell you what type of day it was, I just remember getting in my car and saying OK Lord we have to settle this. Starting the engine, the CD from Kenneth and Gloria Copeland on LOVE confessions started, and God so clearly talked to me, so very strong it was like we were having this conversation. He would say something, then I would ask something and He would answer me. That is when I got my knowing that was deep in my heart, knowing the Love of God. I had played and read that a hundred times, never with such Anointing, but the word of God was so very much alive. When I needed God, He was right with me every step of the way. I knew for sure at that moment everything was right, I remembered what God said.

He says in His word in Isaiah "I the LORD speak righteousness, I declare things that are right." (Isaiah 45:19 KJV) Amen Lord!!!

The results were in, it was not cancer, but we knew that! Walking out of the office the sun shining the air clear and fresh and the glory of God who loves us, the power of His Love was manifested.

Jesus said:

If ye abide in me, and my words abide in you, ye shall ask what ye will, and it shall be done unto you. Herein is my Father glorified, that ye bear much fruit; so shall ye be my disciples. As the Father hath loved me, so have I loved you: continue ye in my love. If ye keep my commandments, ye shall abide in my love; even as I have kept my Father's commandments, and abide in his love. These things have I spoken unto you, that my joy might remain in you, and that your joy might be full.

John 15:7-11 (KJV)

Glory to God

To the Glory of God, my mother, who could not take more than a step, if that, is able, with assistance to move around a little at times, and we are praying every day and night, reading the word of God to her and going over all the benefits she has as a child of God. She is increasing in the knowledge of His Love. I am confident that without God's help I would not be able to care for my mother and the needs that she has, knowing that it is only by His Grace I am able to do for my mother as I do. Understand and know this: It is God being in this place, without him doing and helping, I could not do the things that need to be done. It is all through His ability that I am able. With His Love and strength I have overcoming victory living on the inside of me. It is He who I am thankful and grateful to. He alone needs to be thanked. Each day I in turn am blessed to serve God to bring His healing love.

Do not look at the circumstances look to God who is "LOVE".

Psalm 46 reads: "Be still, and know that I am God: I will be exalted among the heathen, I will be exalted in the earth. The Lord of hosts is with us; the God of Jacob is our refuge. Selah." (Psalm 46:10-11 KJV)

"Be still", I looked up still in Strong's concordance, the root says to mend, physician, heal, repair, thoroughly make whole. You could read it this way;

Be thoroughly made whole, and KNOW I am God who is Love: I will be exalted among the heathen; I will be exalted in the earth. The Lord of hosts is with us; the God of Jacob is our refuge. Selah.

Please do not just leave things up to fate; you may say the results were already in what could you do then? Never stop until it is settled between you and God, and you have a clear understanding, then you stand on that understanding that KNOWING, it could be an hour, a day or 10 years, when you have done all, stand. The enemy would love to eat your lunch and take every bit of it but you can stop him, even as I am writing this I have thoughts of who even cares, do you really think anyone would read this? Oh my friend Yes I do believe, God cares and that is enough for me. By knowing God, His word and all that we have in Christ we always overcome.

Know God's Love first hand!

> Henceforth I call you not servants; for the servant knoweth not what his lord doeth: but I have called you friends; for all things that I have heard of my Father I have made known unto you. Ye have not chosen me, but I have chosen you, and ordained you, that ye should go and bring forth fruit, and that your fruit should remain: that whatsoever ye shall ask of the Father in my name, he may give it you These things I command you, that ye love one another.
>
> John 15:15-17 (KJV)

Chapter 5

OUR FAITH COVENANT WITH GOD

In praying, my response is to follow the promptings of the Holy Spirit, so in faith we are pressing in on our interview with Jesus.

Jesus, it seems that most of our trouble that we experience is from not knowing or fully understanding the truth of all you did and the Love that the Father has for His children. Jesus, what insight would you bring in to our understanding?

Our Covenant with God.

> Even as Abraham believed God, and it was accounted to him for righteousness. Know ye therefore that they which are of faith, the same are the children of

Abraham. And the scripture, foreseeing that God would justify the heathen through faith, preached before the gospel unto Abraham, saying, In thee shall all nations be blessed. So then they which be of faith are blessed with faithful Abraham. For as many as are of the works of the law are under the curse: for it is written, Cursed is every one that continues not in all things which are written in the book of the law to do them. But that no man is justified by the law in the sight of God, it is evident: for, The just shall live by faith. And the law is not of faith: but, The man that doeth them shall live in them. Christ hath redeemed us from the curse of the law, being made a curse for us: for it is written, Cursed is every one that hangeth on a tree: That the blessing of Abraham might come on the Gentiles through Jesus Christ; that we might receive the promise of the Spirit through faith. Brethren, I speak after the manner of men; Though it be but a man's covenant, yet if it be confirmed, no man disannulleth, or addeth thereto. Now to Abraham and his seed were the promises made. He saith not, And to seeds, as of many; but as of one, And to thy seed, which is Christ. And this I say, that the covenant, that was confirmed before of God in Christ, the law, which was four hundred and thirty years after, cannot disannul, that it should make the promise of none effect. For if the inheritance be of the law, it is no more of promise: but God gave it to Abraham by promise. Wherefore then serve the law? It was added because of transgressions, till the seed should come to whom the promise was made; and it was ordained by angels in the hand of a mediator. Now a mediator is not a mediator of one, but God is one. (In the AMP it reads Is the law then against the promises of God? God forbid: for if there had been a law given which could have given life, verily righteousness should have been by the law. But the scripture hath concluded all under sin, that the promise by faith of Jesus Christ might be given to them that, believe. But before faith came, we were kept under the law, shut up unto the faith which should afterwards be revealed. Wherefore the law was our schoolmaster to bring us unto Christ, that we might be justified by faith. But after that faith is come, we are no longer under a schoolmaster. For ye are all the children of God by faith in Christ Jesus. For as many of you as have been baptized into Christ have put on Christ. There is neither Jew nor Greek, there is neither bond nor free, there is neither male nor female: for ye are all one in Christ Jesus. And if ye be Christ's, then are ye Abraham's seed, and heirs according to the promise.

Galatians 3:6-29 (KJV)

I realize this is a power packed chapter full of wonderful words of revelation that the Spirit of God placed in the heart of the Apostle Paul. This will be part of our stepping stones into our better revelation we have through Christ Jesus, The Lord.

As Abraham believed God, and it was accounted to him for righteousness. Clearly stated, how Abraham believed and trusted God the Promisor not the promise. Although it is vital to possess the knowledge of the promises, you have to trust and believe the promisor. A promise is only as sure as the one who promised. To know what we have in Christ through His death and resurrection, is to know all our benefits that the Love of the Father has provided us. Your Faith should not be on just the promise, but on the Promisor. To come to the knowledge of God's Love,and to trust His Love in every area of our life. The love and trust we have in The Almighty God and Father, who is Love, is what brings the promise to life. Faith works by Love. It is God's Love for you when you know and believe in Him.

"So then they which BE of faith are blessed with faithful Abraham." (Galatians 3:9 KJV) Those of FAITH are blessed with faithful Abraham. That would be me and you if you are of Faith, If you believe the Promisor.

Before Christ they worked to sacrifice in order to be accounted as children of the most High God. But it is not works that please God but our faith in Him, for without faith it is imposable to please the Father.

> For as many as are of the works of the law are under the curse: for it is written, Cursed is every one that continueth not in all things which are written in

the book of the law to do them. But that no man is justified by the law in the sight of God, it is evident: for, the just shall live by faith. And the law is not of faith: but, the man that doeth them shall live in them. Christ hath redeemed us from the curse of the law, being made a curse for us: for it is written, Cursed is every one that hangeth on a tree:

Galatians 3:10-13 (kjv)

So then you are not under the law and the curse, you are under the Grace and the Blessing.

The Old Covenant shows or reveals bondage in Galatians 2:16.

The Better Covenant or New Covenant Brings Liberty in 2 Corinthians 3:7.

Old Covenant, by works in Galatians 3:10 and New Covenant by Faith in Galatians 3:11.

The Father and Abraham interned that Covenant several years before the law, but the promises remained; in fact God spelled it out very clearly in Deuteronomy 28.

Simply stated; the law or rules came in to being because of transgressions, until the seed who is Jesus Christ should come to whom the promise was made. It is only through Jesus Christ that we have anything, The Promise to The Seed who is Jesus, you must BE in Christ, without being Christ's, you do not receive the Blessing, all sin, sickness, horror and evil remain, the curse remains, you have and are nothing without being first Christ's! "Wherefore then serveth the law? It was added because of transgressions, till the seed should come to whom the promise was made;" (Galatians 3:19 KJV)

And it was ordained by angels in the hand of a mediator. That God Himself is mediator, before the creation. You do not receive life or become the righteousness of God by law or works (least any man should boast) "But the scripture hath concluded all under sin, that the promise by faith of Jesus Christ might be given to them that believe." (Galatians 3:22 KJV) You are only asked to believe; then and only then are you made the righteousness of God through Christ Jesus.

> For ye are all the children of God by faith in Christ Jesus. For as many of you as have been baptized into Christ have put on Christ. If so you are the seed of Abraham and heir to the Promises, All are His. There is neither Jew nor Greek, there is neither bond nor free, there is neither male nor female: for ye are all one in Christ Jesus. And if ye be Christ's, then are ye Abraham's seed, and heirs according to the promise.
>
> Galatians 3:26-29 (KJV)

Christ has redeemed you from the curse of the law, being made a curse for you. That The Blessing of Abraham would come on you. You receive the promise of the Spirit through faith being Abraham's seed through Jesus and heir according to this promise.

So I asked the Lord; OK I have You and the Father and Holy Spirit why do I need Abraham?

Why Abraham?

He revealed that you can't just take a part of the truth and only walk in just part. If you do, then even that part is incomplete. You are to walk in total victory, Spirit, Soul and Body. You are to prosper in all areas spiritual, physical, and financial. Satan would that you not know all that the Blessing covers. Then you would be less likely to fall for his lies. To know the love of God you have to receive all the blessing not just a part of it.

It is like building a house, you lay your foundation and we all agree you have to have a good foundation. But the home is not complete, you add the frame work and it still is not done. You dry it in and it still is not done, you finish the outside with brick and a 40 year roof, but it still is not done. Sure you can live in it, should it rain, you will not get wet. It is still just the outer shell; the place you would live is void missing all the essentials of life, empty.

If it turns cold and you have no heater, you will be ok if the temperature does not drop too much. If it does how will you keep warm or in the summer, how will you cool off? You diligently work in the yard and the outside looks wonderful. Continually working on the outside; on your yard, you toil to keep every weed out and everything in its rightful place, all in order. Then you become hungry and need to eat to restore your strength. You have no kitchen, therefore, no place to cook or eat, and what about rest, how will you find rest? You have no place to lay your head, when day is done, when your body needs nourishment and refreshing of a hot shower to wash off your day, you find none.

> Through wisdom is an house builded; and by understanding it is established: And by knowledge shall the chambers be filled with all precious and pleasant riches.
>
> Proverbs 24:3-4 (KJV)

The Holy Spirit is ready to refresh and restore, the Blood of Jesus washes and brings healing and God Himself gives us peace. The Lord is the one that gives you the power to get wealth. You think your home is built and that my friend is how the enemy works, to keep as much truth out and away from you so you will not walk in all the Glory, all the power, all the victory, all the health, all the prosperity, that Jesus paid so very dearly for. You may even start looking to things or people to fill the needs you have, needs that God created you to have, needs only His LOVE fulfills.

That is one of the tricks the enemy uses, you can't think your way. You will have to take all the truth, all the Lords ways and to know His way you have to read His word.

My question rendered this. The curse was brought in by sin and that sin brought with it death of all living things, all of mankind that included spiritual and tangible things.

Think about it, most everything, if not everything made comes from the earth.

When Adam and Eve were in the garden and they knew no sin, they had The Father's Glory and Love to keep them, they only knew things that were right and good. When you don't know the truth of God's Glory and Love what will keep you?

For God Himself said in Isaiah "For thus saith the Lord that created the heavens;

> God himself that formed the earth and made it; he hath established it, he created it not in vain, he formed it to be inhabited: I am the Lord; and there is none else. I have not spoken in secret, in a dark place of the earth: I said not unto the seed of Jacob, Seek ye me in vain: I the Lord speak righteousness, I declare things that are right.
>
> Isaiah 45:18-19 (KJV)

He created all things for us to inhabit.

When death came it brought all darkness, not only to the soul and spirit man, but to his body, his possessions, the very ground he walks on. Death and sin the offence.

> For as by one man's disobedience many were made sinners, so by the obedience of one shall many be made righteous. Moreover the law entered, that the offence might abound. But where sin abounded, grace did much more abound: That as sin hath

reigned unto death, even so might grace reign through righteousness unto eternal life by Jesus Christ our Lord.

Romans 5:19-21 (KJV)

But not as the offence, so also is the free gift. For if through the offence of one many be dead, much more the grace of God, and the gift by grace, which is by one man, Jesus Christ, hath abound unto many.

The curse covered all mankind, so then Christ's redemption not only removes the curse, He set you free from the law of sin and death!!! Took it out of the way, nailing it to His cross, all that it brought with it, that is why you need to comprehend, study, research and understand that it is not only spiritual but also physical redemption; all God's children should know what free gift of Grace they have in Christ's death and resurrection!

When I asked Jesus that, in my heart I heard "I want you to prosper in all areas of your life that all grace abound toward you; that you, always have all sufficiency in all things, may abound to every good work: To know the promises I promised with the covenant cross and all that the Cross did for all mankind. I want My people to walk in the knowledge that I will never leave them, that you will always be able to count on Me being there for you and that I take your part, I am on your right side always and My Glory is your rear guard. I come that you might have life and have it more abundant."

Praise you Jesus!

God said to Abram, this is God speaking ears up please; after these things the word of the Lord came unto Abram in a vision, saying, "Fear not, Abram: I am thy shield, and thy exceeding great reward." (Genesis 15:1 KJV) Glory to God!!!!

Fear not. You can't just tell someone don't fear and then not remove the sting fear brings. God through His Covenant removes that sting of fear through faith in the Promisor and the power thereof. He himself is our Shield, that I have personally experienced in my own life. And talk about reward, there is nothing any greater, as written thy exceeding great reward.

So then, would God want you to prosper? Would God want you to walk in health? Would God want you to bring the Gospel, the Good News to others? Does God want you to have Peace? How about Joy unspeakable? The list could go on for days. I would say the answer to all this is YES, YES, YES!

Keep your Faith on THE PROMISOR not the promise, knowing His promise, reading the word, users in the heart, His love for you, this free gift of God. Keeping in your heart the Giver of this free gift to you and the horrendous price He paid.

For the Giver of a gift, is the one who pays the price of the gift. As glorious and unable to be measured as the gift is, it is not the gift; it is the Giver of the gift that is important, for without the Giver you have no gift. Established in Faith you believing in Christ Jesus and receive all the Promise from God. You receive the promise of the Spirit through faith being Abraham's seed through Jesus and heir to the promise.

Abraham believed God.

"For what saith the scripture? Abraham believed God, and it was counted unto him for righteousness". (Romans 4:3 KJV)

"Even as Abraham believed God, and it was accounted to him for righteousness." (Galatians 3:3 KJV)

"And the scripture was fulfilled which saith, Abraham believed God, and it was imputed unto him for righteousness: and he was called the Friend of God." (James 2:23 KJV)

Do you believe God?

Chapter 6

PUREST LOVE "JESUS"

The Word of God tells us that after Adam and Eve sinned the curse came on all mankind. The Word of God also tells us that Jesus took that curse on Himself. That He was made sin.

"For he hath made him to be sin for us, who knew no sin; that we might be made the righteousness of God in him."(2 Corinthians 5:21 KJV)

Jesus took that curse and took it all the way to the cross and He did not stop there He took it all the way to hell and spoiled.....

Let's stop and look at the word spoiled In the Strong's Concordance the root of it in the Greek

> Pronunciation *apo'* a primary particle; "off," i.e. away (from something near), in various senses (of place, time, or relation; literal or figurative. In composition (as a prefix) it usually denotes separation, departure,

cessation, completion, reversal, also the root word, Pronunciation *ek-doo'-o*to cause to sink out (specially as of clothing) to divest:—strip, take off from, unclothe.

Strong's Concordance

Dictionary (sink a process that absorb or remove energy or a substance to swallow whole)

Let's say it this way Jesus through the power of The Holy Spirit; cause to sink, strip off, to strip, swallow up, divest, take off from, and unclothe the authority Adam gave when he sinned. Jesus Himself with the power from on high; denotes separation, departure, cessation, stopping or halt put a stop to, completion it is done, reversal to change back into the hands of the Creator!!!!!

Reversal to change back into the hands of the Creator!!!!! That was worth saying twice Glory!!!

I can only imagine, as the heavens looked on; Glory what a sight to see.

Imagine, seeing David and Moses, Abraham, Eli, Samuel, Nathan, Elijah, Elisha, Job, Joel, Jonah, Amos, Enoch, Isaiah, Micah, Nahum, Zephaniah, Jeremiah, Habakkuk, Obadiah, Daniel, Ezekiel, Haggai, Malachi, the list goes on.

All the heavenly hosts of Angels as they cheered Jesus on to Glory! The Power of Love manifested His overcoming ability through The Holy Spirit, Love who created all things in Love, triumphs to Victory!!!

As they saw Jesus make a show of them openly having spoiled principalities and powers triumphing over them in it. !!!!!!!

Praise, Glory, Honor!

Blessing and honor and glory and power be unto Him.

The Word says it all "Blotting out the handwriting of ordinances that was against us, which was contrary to us, and took it out of the way, nailing it to his cross; And having spoiled principalities and powers, he made a shew of them openly, triumphing over them in it." (Colossians 2:14-15 KJV)

Paul so confidently says; "O death, where is thy sting? O grave, where is thy victory?" (1 Corinthians 15:55 KJV)

The more you know and understand the word of God, the Love of God and all that you have in Christ, you too will know the Authority Jesus gives us in His Name.

"So when this corruptible shall have put on incorruption, and this mortal shall have put on immortality, then shall be brought to pass the saying that is written, Death is swallowed up in victory." (1 Corinthians 15:54 KJV)

Glory…….. Praise The Lord God!!

Jesus took back everything that evil took. Every chain has been broken Satan has no power over you, only if he convinces you to think he has. Look very close at that chain, it is already broken, it is just laying on you. Shake it off, let go, give it to Jesus, lay it back on His cross and don't pick it back up. Start shaking off the chains that evil tries to hold you down with, read the word of God and see what God has to say about you. My dear friend He paid a tremendous price for you and me, freely, to give you all that the Father intended.

Jesus said; "No man taketh it from me, but I lay it down of myself. I have power to lay it down, and I have power to take it again. This commandment have I received of my Father." (John 10:18 KJV)

Let's not walk from crises to crises or from miracle to miracle, but let us walk the walk of Faith so we can go from faith to faith and from Glory to Glory, as God ordained.

Stop and look at your home, how's it looking? Remember that same Power that raised Christ Jesus from the dead lives inside of you, if you are a believer. Do you have some unfinished rooms? Is it time to decorate? All you need is Jesus I am confident you will never find a better carpenter.

As we continue on, Jesus will uncover more truths to us and so we shall build on.

I have to stop and Praise and thank God, what an Awesome God we serve!!!!! For as I am writing this I am also being awestruck, blessed and my spirit wants to stand up and shout and dance to the Glory of God. Let's Dance!

Thank you my Sweet Jesus, thank You, thank You. I love you ☺

You are my Purest Love "Jesus"

Chapter 7

COVENANT WITH GOD

Looking at the Covenant with God and Abram, you see Abram's heart. In Genesis chapter 14 he overcame the battle. He returned triumphant to be greeted by the king of Sodom who went out to meet him after his return from the slaughter of Chedorlaomer, and of the kings that were with him, at the valley of Shaveh. And Melchizedek, king of Salem, brought forth bread and wine: he was the priest of the most high God. And Melchizedek blessed Abram as the blessed of the most high God. Abram gave to Melchizedek tithes of all that they had gotten.

The king of Sodom wanted only the people and wanted to give Abram the rest of what he brought back with them. But that was not Abram's heart, his heart was with God, he said no thanks, just give only that which the young men have eaten, and the portion of the men which went with me,

Aner, Eshcol, and Mamre and let them take their portion.
Abram gave his tithes and to his servants their portion but
for himself, he wanted nothing from them. He said to the
king of Sodom," I have lift up mine hand unto the Lord,
the most high God, the possessor of heaven and earth that
I will not take from a thread even to a shoe latchet, and that
I will not take any thing that is yours, lest you should say, I
have made Abram rich" This was between God and Abram
his personal walk with God. It was what Abram had talked
to God himself about from his own heart to God's.

We then read what God said to Abram, after these
things the word of the Lord came unto Abram in a vision,
saying, Fear not, Abram: I am thy shield, and thy exceeding
great reward. Glory to God, God just gave Himself to
Abram and yet he said I have no seed. Abram's reward
is God Himself and his shield, yet still his desire in the
word is for a seed, a child. Could it be that he was so very
confident in God's love for him that what God just told
him, Abram thought, I know but, what could you give me
in this world that would really matter, I know I have you.
Could it be that Abram so wanted this deep desire of his
heart he walked right over the GREAT Blessing God just
gave him, I say either way we can learn from this. It does
not talk about Abrams reaction to the vision other than
Abram shows to God his true desire. All the gifts he could
get from God would not replace or fulfill the desire for a
child. But what does Abram's heart show; it is not about

money and riches gold and silver. Abram didn't have the book to read as we do for his life, he could not go to the chapter that tells of all God did. No, he had to walk in FAITH to ask God what will you give me? I have no seed what does it matter? Abram then had to trust that God will do as He says.

We know, from the word of God, what God did, we know what God had in store for Abram to make him Abraham the father of many nations. Do you sometimes look past the blessing right in front of you, and not take the blessing right in your hands but look for what you don't have yet? You may not have a book written on your life with chapter and verse to see what is next, but neither did Abraham or Moses. What you do have is God's WORD to hold on to, which will take you from faith to faith and glory to glory.

You have the truth for your life and the promises of God. You, in faith in Christ can take your blessing, as God Himself has given to you Jesus, The Holy Spirit and Himself, as your shield deliverer and your exceeding great reward walking each day, one day at a time. Can you trust Him for the rest of the story of your life?

Abram's greatest desire was to have a seed a child, look what God did, in satisfying the desire of Abrams heart. I would call that no small thing, he wanted a seed over material things and look what God gave him.

God blessed Abraham. "And he brought him forth abroad, and said, Look now toward heaven, and tell the stars, if thou be able to number them: and he said unto him, So shall thy seed be. And he believed in the Lord; and he counted it to him for righteousness. (Genesis 15:5-6 KJV)

God will if you let Him, do the same for you. God wants to give you your hearts desires. Our Great and Awesome God is no small giver, if you look at all He has given and continues to give, it by far out does anything you could ever ask or think. Abraham desires to be a father more than gold or silver, God gives him to be a father to Nation's!!!!

> Many, O Lord my God, are thy wonderful works which thou hast done, and thy thoughts which are to us-ward: they cannot be reckoned up in order unto thee: if I would declare and speak of them, they are more than can be numbered.
>
> Psalm 40:5 (KJV)

Remembering your very greatest gift is Jesus your Savior and Lord your Redeemer.

> After these things the word of the Lord came unto Abram in a vision, saying, Fear not, Abram: I am thy shield, and thy exceeding great reward. And Abram said, Lord God, what wilt thou give me, seeing I go childless, and the steward of my house is this Eliezer of Damascus? And Abram said, Behold, to me thou hast given no seed: and, lo, one born in

my house is mine heir. And, behold, the word of the Lord came unto him, saying, this shall not be thine heir; but he that shall come forth out of thine own bowels shall be thine heir. And he brought him forth abroad, and said, Look now toward heaven, and tell the stars, if thou be able to number them: and he said unto him, So shall thy seed be. And he believed in the Lord; and he counted it to him for righteousness. And he said unto him, I am the Lord that brought thee out of Ur of the Chaldees, to give thee this land to inherit it. And he said, Lord God, whereby shall I know that I shall inherit it? And he said unto him, Take me an heifer of three years old, and a she goat of three years old, and a ram of three years old, and a turtledove, and a young pigeon. And he took unto him all these, and divided them in the midst, and laid each piece one against another: but the birds divided he not. And when the fowls came down upon the carcases, Abram drove them away. And when the sun was going down, a deep sleep fell upon Abram; and, lo, an horror of great darkness fell upon him. And he said unto Abram, Know of a surety that thy seed shall be a stranger in a land that is not theirs, and shall serve them; and they shall afflict them four hundred years; And also that nation, whom they shall serve, will I judge: and afterward shall they come out with great substance. And thou shalt go to thy fathers in peace; thou shalt be buried in a good old age. But in the fourth generation they shall come hither again: for the iniquity of the Amorites is not yet full. And it came to pass, that, when the sun went down, and it was dark, behold a smoking furnace, and a burning lamp that passed between those pieces. In the same day the Lord made a covenant with Abram, saying, Unto thy seed have I given this land, from the river of Egypt unto the great river, the river Euphrates:

Genesis 15:1-18 (KJV)

God made this covenant the promise of the Cross. He swore to it He will not break the covenant.

"God is not a man, that he should lie; neither the son of man, that he should repent: hath he said, and shall he not do it? or hath he spoken, and shall he not make it good?" (Numbers 23:19 KJV)

Nevertheless My loving-kindness will I not utterly take from him, nor suffer my faithfulness to fail. My covenant will I not break, nor alter the thing that is gone out of my lips. Once have I sworn by my holiness that I will not lie unto David. His seed shall endure forever, and his throne as the sun before me. It shall be established for ever as the moon, and as a faithful witness in heaven. Selah.

Psalm 89:33-37 (KJV)

So it would be to your benefit to know and understand your benefits of God's Covenant. Abram asked God "And he said, Lord God, whereby shall I know that I shall inherit it?" (Genesis 15:8 ᴋᴊᴠ) So God cut the Covenant which is the fore coming of our better Covenant in Christ of His cross, whereby it is complete, done restored back, and sin and death have no place in the believer. You have been redeemed, by the Blood of Jesus.

You all know that Satan is a liar; and he will use anything and everything to trick you. You will know he will even use the word of God; in fact, it worked with Eve. If Satan can keep you in doubt of what the Word says and your mind on the wrong you may think you have done, and not on what the word says or that Jesus paid in full the price needed for your redemption. Satan will try to keep you from walking in the faith you have in Christ and he is able to steal the Glory God has for you.

But the word of God says;

> For I am persuaded, that neither death, nor life, nor angels, nor principalities, nor powers, nor things present, nor things to come, Nor height, nor depth, nor any other creature, shall be able to separate us from the love of God, which is in Christ Jesus our Lord.
>
> Romans 8:38-39 (ᴋᴊᴠ)

Let's look at just a few examples of how the word has been watered down to keep God's people from fully understanding who they are in Christ and what they have to help walk this walk of Faith through love.

Christians are called peculiar people, so laugh and say yes we are a strange and odd people and then say; oh I like being odd if it is for God. But what does God say!!!!!!!

> And the LORD hath avouched thee this day to be his peculiar people, as he hath promised thee, and that thou shouldest keep all his commandments; And to make thee high above all nations which he hath made, in praise, and in name, and in honor; and that thou may be an holy people unto the LORD thy God, as he hath spoken.
>
> Deut. 26:18-19 (KJV)

"For thou art an holy people unto the LORD thy God, and the LORD hath chosen thee to be a peculiar people unto himself, above all the nations that are upon the earth." (Deuteronomy 14:2 KJV)

The Hebrew Old Testament word is "gulla" and it is saying treasured possession.

> But ye are a chosen generation, a royal priesthood, an holy nation, a peculiar people; that ye should show forth the praises of him who hath called you out of darkness into his marvelous light; (Praise God!) Which in time past were not a people, but are now the people of God: which had not obtained mercy, but now have obtained mercy.
>
> 1 Peter 2:9-10 (KJV)

The Greek New Testament word is "peripoiesis" posses-sion, property, sharing in, gaining, purchased possession.

Jesus paid a tremendous price to purchase God's treasured possession. To God we are a treasured possession, how cool is that?

> By having the eyes of your heart flooded with light, so that you can know and understand the hope to which He has called you, and how rich is His glorious inheritance in the saints (His set-apart ones), And [so that you can know and understand] what is the immeasurable and unlimited and surpassing greatness of His power in and for us who believe, as demonstrated in the working of His mighty strength, Which He exerted in Christ when He raised Him from the dead and seated Him at His [own] right hand in the heavenly [places],
>
> Ephesians 1:18-20 (KJV)

We, His Church, belong to God and being God's, His Holy People through faith in Christ, we have Hope to which He has called you and rich is His glorious inheritance. We are a holy people set apart, chosen generation, a royal priesthood an holy nation into his marvelous light !!! That is how God thinks of us.

You hear all the time people say; "have the peace that passes all understanding", but that is not what the word of God says; it says

And the peace of God, which passes all understanding, shall keep your hearts and minds through Christ Jesus.

It is God's peace that shall keep your hearts and minds through Christ which passes all understanding.

> Jesus answered and said unto him, If a man love me, he will keep my words: and my Father will love him, and we will come unto him, and make our abode with him. He that loveth me not keepeth not my sayings: and the word which ye hear is not mine, but the Father's which sent me. These things have I spoken unto you, being yet present with you. But the Comforter, which is the Holy Ghost, whom the Father will send in my name, he shall teach you all things, and bring all things to your remembrance, whatsoever I have said unto you. Peace I leave with you, my peace I give unto you: not as the world giveth, give I unto you. Let not your heart be troubled, neither let it be afraid. Ye have heard how I said unto you, I go away, and come again unto you. If ye loved me, ye would rejoice, because I said, I go unto the Father: for my Father is greater than I.
>
> John 14:23-28 (KJV)

You also hear" God doesn't give you more than you can take or handle" then you somehow make a joke of it and think I must be strong cause He sure is loading it on. But what is the word saying? First of all it is talking about a Temptation, not trouble or sickness or financial problems;

It says "There hath no temptation taken you but such as is common to man: but God is faithful, who will not suffer you to be tempted above that ye are able; but will with the temptation also make a way to escape, that ye may be able to bear it." (1 Corinthians 10:13 KJV)

Let's look at the word temptation; the act of tempting; enticement or allurement. Something that tempts, entices, or allures. A fact or state of being tempted, especially to do evil.

Hello! God does not tempt us!!!

This kind of thinking leads you to think God is giving you all these bad things; sickness, family trouble, poverty, brokenness, desire to sin; the list goes on. And that you are the one that is going to have to do the overcoming. Thinking like this takes your mind off the real overcoming POWER, The Word of God. And if a temptation to sin comes at you, you think I just can't do it, or you try in your own strength and it doesn't work. You don't have to; it is Christ in you and the word of God that is your SOURCE of POWER.

> I am the true vine, and my Father is the husbandman. Every branch in me that beareth not fruit he taketh away: and every branch that beareth fruit, he purgeth it, that it may bring forth more fruit. Now ye are clean through the word which I have spoken unto you. Abide in me, and I in you. As the branch cannot bear fruit of itself, except it abide in the vine;

no more can ye, except ye abide in me. I am the vine, ye are the branches: He that abideth in me, and I in him, the same bringeth forth much fruit: for without me ye can do nothing.

John 15:1-5 (KJV)

I was raised in upstate New York around the great lakes; we would go for drives and certain times of year we would go to Watkins Glen and the farmlands to pick Cherries and Grapes. Talk about a marvelous time, I would find a "great cherry tree" and prop myself up in it and eat the fruit till it was time to leave. Needless to say my pail was not full when it was time to go. My father would say we will have to start weighing you before we start and then again after. Anyways; in the vineyard's the vine dresser who cared for the vines would walk the vineyard's and carefully look things over. If he found a branch laying on the ground, he knew it would not be able to produce fruit, so he would gently raise the branch up and he would brace the branch with the needed support, and then that branch would in fact produce fruit. We have a loving and tender caring God, who Satan does not want you to realize how LOVING He is.

The word says that There hath no temptation taken you but such as is common to man. So with fellowship one to another in the love of God, the word of God in your heart, the blood of Jesus, you are able to overcome. It says God is faithful and able to make a way of escape. God would not tempt you and then give you a way out, God is not the one tempting you to sin or to fall short of the glory. He is not the tempter, but will in fact provide a way out. Glory be to God.

Ok let me go all the way out on this limb, giving you one more. This may stir up some controversy. Now I am going to get into a lie that a religion was partly founded on and some of the doctrine of it. Yet it is preached in several different denominations.

In today's message not all but a great number, it is preached "Peter" was the rock that the church was built on. I understand that for years this was taught like this. I do however now believe that is not what Jesus was saying. He, JESUS was asking the apostles who they think that He is.

And Peter speaks up and says "Thou art The Christ, the Son of the living God"

God Himself brought truth to Peter He revealed truth of who Jesus is. This is a very BIG deal this is Jesus the Savior the Christ!!!! We are talking, son of God Himself.

Jesus was saying, He is the Rock, this Truth, He will build His church on. He is the Christ the Son of the living God, the only rock or foundation that the gates of hell cannot prevail over.

On Aug. 23, 2010 The Lord through the Holy Spirit showed me this in Matthew.

Jesus said unto them "But whom say ye that I am?" (Matthew 16:15 KJV)

And Simon Peter answered and said, "Thou art The Christ, the Son of the living God." (Matthew 16:16 KJV)

And Jesus answered and said unto him. "Blessed art thou, Simon Barjona: for flesh and blood hath not revealed it unto thee, but my Father which is in heaven." (Matthew 16:17 KJV)

Then Jesus goes on to say, "And I say also unto thee thou art Peter, and upon this rock I will build My church and the gates of hell shall not prevail against it". (Matthew 16:18 KJV)

> The word in Strong's Concordance is
>
> Peter = in v17 when translated from Strong's is "Petros or rock that is stone, rock or individual stone."
>
> Rock = in v 18 when translated from Strong's is "Petra or bedrock or large rock formation, suitable solid foundation contrast to individual stone."
>
> (Strong's Concordance)

You may try reading it like this;

And I say also unto you of this (truth that My Father revealed) as sure as you are Peter upon this rock (or foundation or this truth) I the Christ will build my Church and the gates of hell shall not prevail against the Christ the Son of the Living God!!!!!

or

And I say also unto you of this Peter (Rock Petros); upon this rock (bedrock foundation Petra), I will build my Church and the gates of hell shall not prevail against it.

Then if you read what Jesus says to his disciples in verse "Then charged he his disciples that they should tell no man that he was Jesus the Christ." (Matthew 16:20 KJV)

Jesus is connecting back to the question who do you say I am, and the statement Peter said "the Christ" this truth who Jesus is, the Christ the Messiah, when Jesus says and the gates of hell cannot over take us because Jesus gives us the keys of the Kingdome of heaven, but tell no man that He is the Messiah. Why? Because He has to walk through the purpose the fulfillment of why Jesus came. He then talked to them about what would have to come to pass.

Please note that in verse 23, Peter lets Satan talk.

> From that time forth began Jesus to shew unto his disciples, how that he must go unto Jerusalem, and suffer many things of the elders and chief priests and scribes, and be killed, and be raised again the third day. Then Peter took him (JESUS), and began to rebuke him, saying, Be it far from thee, Lord: this shall not be unto thee. But he (JESUS) turned, and said unto Peter, Get thee behind me, Satan: thou art an offence unto me: for thou savourest not the things that be of God, but those that be of men.
>
> Matthew 6:21-25 (KJV)

This is the foundation "God" is going to build His Church on and the gates of hell can get in. It can only be Jesus He is our only foundation any other will not stand.

> Therefore whosoever heareth these sayings of mine, and doeth them, I will liken him unto a wise man, which built his house upon a rock: And the rain descended, and the floods came, and the winds blew, and beat upon that house; and it fell not: for it was founded upon a rock.
>
> Matthew 6:24-25 (KJV)

Each time rock in v 25 = from Strong's Concordance is Petra or bedrock or large rock formation, suitable solid foundation

Peter, in v 23= translated from Strong's Concordance is Petros or rock that is stone, rock or individual

When we look through all scripture we see our rock is Jesus Christ The foundation of God.

"He is the Rock, his work is perfect: for all his ways are judgment; a God of truth and without iniquity, just and right is he." (Deuteronomy 32:4 KJV)

Please don't just take my word, research this for yourself. In fact you should always research the word of God for confirmation of a truth or teaching.

Is this truth important? You tell me, think about it……..

Most of you know the passage in Jeremiah "For I know the thoughts or some versions say plans that I think toward you, said the Lord, thoughts of peace, and not of evil, to give you an expected end." (Jeremiah 29:11 KJV) And we all want to be in God's plan for us. We read all kinds of books to get us in God's perfect place for our life. That is all well and good, but the enemy uses this to keep your mind on what you think is a failure.

What does the word say? What kind of thoughts or plans, of peace not evil, if you dwell on the things that didn't turn out the way "you thought" they should, you will miss the "blessing" in that situation. Then you think: what a mess I made. Can God make it work? Can He clean up this mess? So you keep looking at the situation. How it didn't turn out like you thought it should. Did I not stay in God's plan? You thought you did right if only... Then you are left questioning yourself, you are then double minded and unstable in all you do. "A double minded man is unstable in all his ways." (James 1:8 KJV) That is exactly where Satan wants you. You then may sit in it and say am I ever going to get it? You may think it is going to take a lifetime to repair if ever. You may even think you have to do or should have done something differently. Oh yes, if you would have, could have, and should have, keeps coming up. You repent, let go, let God but why does it keep coming back? You keep thinking and dwelling on the things that could have been and don't take the time to look for the blessings.

We all want the vision God has for us, but sometimes God doesn't give it to you right away. Let me explain one way. The Lord puts desires in our heart of things He would have you do. You can and should be obedient to this calling, yet He may not give you a full picture or a vision, you may only get stepping stones.

This is what the Lord gave me stepping stones. He gave me assignments to do and I did what He placed in my heart. Of the many different assignments that He placed in my heart, one was to be a Pastor. So I studied and did as He said, but no vision. At the time I was doing prison ministry. Then He placed on my heart to check out jail ministry, but no true vision.

Please note, other people cannot give you your vision. When it comes to your Vision, they can only confirm to you what the Lord has already been talking to you about. Sometimes you may want to know what God has for you, you may actually seek from others this information. I am saying this because others may come and say things out of what they know about you, not out of what the Lord is saying. But check it out, it will bear witness in your spirit. Always check the spirit and know they are from God. God will always place in your heart your vision first, and then others will confirm what you have in your heart.

When He placed in my heart to go to the jails, He opened the door to minister one on one with the inmates. One of the requirements was to be a Pastor, but still I knew there was something more, something, but not sure what it was. Oh I would pray for a vision. He kept me seeking, asking and more seeking, knowing in my heart there is more. I would keep on praying. For years I studied the word of God and all the teaching on the word of God the Spirit led me to; each time the Lord would give me assignments, I would ask the Lord where my vision is? Next thing I knew, the assignment was over. I would pray and pray getting a little glimpse but just a glimpse nothing I could say was my vision. Deep in my heart I have always had a tremendous desire to serve Him ever since I was a child, but no real vision.

When I brought my mother home, I left my job and did what I believe the Lord would have me do. My daughter who lives in Kentucky brought to mind the scripture the Lord had given her, as she is walking through her own walk. It was when Jesus was in the garden and He was praying. When He returned to his disciples and they were sleeping, He said could you not pray just a little while with me? Sometimes we don't understand until it is over but we have to trust Him in all things.

Getting assignments from God, but still did not get a full vision. Then one day as I praying, I received my vision. It is something the Lord and I are working on together now.

Looking back and seeing the glimpses and stepping stones, it all makes perfect sense for me and the way I am. This is how the Lord would have given me my vision, He kept me seeking Him doing all sorts of things for Him, working with young children, then teens, young adults, couples, singles, Christians, in nursing homes, teaching, interceding, working with people of all types of backgrounds in prison, men and women, some who never even knew about God at all, showing the Love of God to them. Still at any time the Spirit leads, ready to intercede and or minister in obedience. He blesses me with so many stepping stones. What tremendous gifts all the blessings on the way, my journey with the Lord, Awesome!

If it is taking you time to get your vision, do not get discouraged. Many times you hear people say; the Lord said; and off they go into full time ministry and that is great. But for me, I didn't get it that way. God gave me one step at a time. At times, I had to pray not to think I was failing, I knew what the word says but we sometimes tire or think we are doing things wrong and God doesn't have that for us. Take each stepping stone at a time until you hear otherwise from the Lord, each step, each assignment is your training ground. God does a lot of on job training. Do not give up, He always does what His Word says. It may take years; I am talking lots of years.

Let me give you an example. We opened a wonderful coffee house, a blessing to all who entered and the Lord was in this place. It was a Christian Coffee house, a very small taste of the Garden, right on the Gulf overlooking the Bay. Faiths of all beliefs came, the Gideon's would come on Saturday mornings, Christian College Students would have Bible Studies, and on Friday nights they would come sing praises to God, and have wonderful fellowship. Jehovah Wittiness would come and sit next to the students all in harmony, many different denominations came. As glorious as this was, it was for a season, and it closed. That was a sad day for me. On the way driving home the day of closing, I asked the Lord why? He said I knew when I placed Adam in the Garden what was to come, but I did it anyway, the end is greater than the first. We talked more He said look at the fruit that came out from this year; it was tremendous, so very much took place so very many lives were touched and helped and changed by the Lords Hand. The Lord was very much in this Place.

When it closed I received all kinds of words from people. One said, "I know you prayed but you got ahead of God." Another one said that "you must have been out of His perfect will." So I said to the Lord, "That is not what You told me, sure I want your perfect will." What I got in my spirit was look at the blessings, not the loss, look at the Glory, and keep your mind on all the wonderful blessings that came out of this calling. So I held on to that and praise God for it. And as always, He lifted me up.

Look at the blessings not the loss, look at the Glory, and keep your mind on all the wonderful blessings that came out of this calling. We have to trust God even when things don't go the way we think they should or end up the way we thought it should be. When you trust God in all the situations of your life, it always works out just right.

Paul was led by The Holy Spirit to write: "And be not conformed to this world: but be ye transformed by the renewing of your mind, that ye may prove what is that good, and acceptable, and perfect, will of God." (Romans 12:2 KJV) We renew our mind, reading the word of God. Taking what He says and not what the world says. Then any time any trouble would come up and the accuser would come at you with a twist of God's word, and you start to think if only I would have…… The Word that you put in your heart by the Spirit of God will turn your thoughts to Him.

You have as Peter said: "gird up the loins of your mind, be sober, and hope to the end for the grace that is to be brought unto you at the revelation of Jesus Christ;" (1 Peter 1:13 KJV)

Let me tell you what the Holy Spirit revealed to me the other day as I was reading the word and I have been meditating on this as The Spirit lead over the past few days.

I was just reading the Word of God. I was not thinking about plans or really anything on that line of thinking, I was in Genesis 25 reading Rebekah became pregnant.

The babies jostled each other within her, and she said, "Why is this happening to me?" So she went to inquire of the Lord. The Lord said to her, "Two nations are in your womb, and two peoples from within you will be separated; one people will be stronger than the other, and the older will serve the younger."

Genesis 25:22-23 (KJV)

Reading on we see that Esau sold his birthright to Jacob and he gave Esau some bread and some lentil stew for his birthright. We also see how Rebekah tricked Isaac into blessing Jacob.

The Spirit said in my heart, God's will is always known and it is not you working out through your wrongs but that God knows before the foundation what you will do the choices we make the things you will do and not do. Nothing surprises Him. We do not have to fit in His plan He has already fit all things together in yours.

For we are saved by hope: but hope that is seen is not hope: for what a man seeth, why doth he yet hope for? But if we hope for that we see not, then do we with patience wait for it. Likewise the Spirit also helpeth our infirmities: for we know not what we should pray for as we ought: but the Spirit itself maketh intercession for us with groanings which cannot be uttered. And he that searcheth the hearts knoweth what is the mind of the Spirit, because he maketh intercession for the saints according to the will of God. And we know that all things work together for good to them that love God, to them who are the called according to his purpose. For whom he did foreknow, he also did predestinate to be conformed to the image of his Son, that he might be the firstborn among many brethren. Moreover whom he did predestinate, them he also called: and whom he called, them he also justified: and whom he justified, them he also glorified. What shall we then say to these things? If God be for us, who can be against us?

(Romans 8:24-31 KJV)

God has not altered your choices, He just knows all that you would ever do and He has a plan that fits everything you have ever done or will do. You still have the right to make choices, but the closer you walk with Him, the stronger your faith in Him becomes, the easier it becomes to be in that right place. If God be for you, who can be against you? I have said I could be doing a thousand things and everyone is in order but if "I" "Try to do something and it is a struggle" I know I better get before God and fast. For me, if it is a struggle I need to check in the word of God and find my Peace.

Also, if things in your life are not going the way you think or would like them to, take it to God in prayer. He is there for you and you will be amazed how He will work it out for your good. So many things are not what they seem to be, good or not so good but with God all things work out and the love of God will lift you up and over even when the circumstances seem to be the same.

Praying for your walk, to know His will for your walk and calling is needed. We are to seek Him.

In Philippians"Do not be anxious about anything, but in every situation by prayer and petition, with thanksgiving, present your requests to God." (Philippians 4:6 KJV) Praying, asking of God, is not begging God; it is making our request known.

For Faith to work, you are to walk in love. Faith works through LOVE that also means you have to love yourself. But you may say; if only I could remove all sin and failure like going back to the Garden; well my friend you can, you can have that IN CHRIST. ALL sin ALL wrong choices all choices made with right intentions, all things that will ever concern you are taken care of. All of that was placed on the cross every last one for all mankind once and for all.

You have to know you are redeemed set free from the curse. Know you are in the Kingdom of God; you are His child created in Christ Jesus unto good works.

"For we are his workmanship, created in Christ Jesus unto good works, which God hath before ordained that we should walk in them." (Ephesians 2:10 KJV)

In reading the word to my mother; "blessed be the Lord, who daily loads us with benefits, even the God of our salvation. Selah." (Psalm 68:19 KJV)

"Bless the LORD, O my soul, and forget not all his benefits" (Psalm 103:2 KJV)

I was shown this about benefits as I was reading this to my mother; my mother was with a company called Corning Glass Works and when she retired she received a benefit package. If you do not know just what is in that package or what you are entitled to receive, you will most likely not use or take advantage of all your benefits. They are there but if you don't accept or know what you have you are not going to benefit from all that you have been given. They have already been packaged already paid for no cost to you. Yours as a member of Corning Glass works, well as joint heirs with Christ, we are in Christ, we are in the Kingdom of God, you and I have the benefits of the Kingdom of God, that were already set forth. In fact we have a better set of benefits because we have a better promise or a better package. We have the complete package the total upgrade.

Jesus gave us a better Covenant.

"But now hath he obtained a more excellent ministry, by how much also he is the mediator of a better covenant, which was established upon better promises." (Hebrews 8:6 KJV)

Why do we say better? Well that is because it was paid in full, placed back in the hands of God the Creator. You can walk in love, as Christ also hath loved us, and hath given himself for us an offering and a sacrifice to God for a sweet smelling savor. For you were sometimes darkness, but now are you light in the Lord: walk as children of light. That ye might walk worthy of the Lord unto all pleasing, being fruitful in every good work, and increasing in the knowledge of God. For as you have therefore received Christ Jesus as your Lord, so you walk in Him.

"For it is not possible that the blood of bulls and of goats should take away sins." (Hebrews 10:4 KJV)

"Neither by the blood of goats and calves, but by his own blood he entered in once into the holy place, having obtained eternal redemption for us." (Hebrews 9:12 KJV) Glory to God!!!

"For sin shall not have dominion over you: for ye are not under the law, but under grace. What then? Shall we sin, because we are not under the law, but under grace? God forbid." (Romans 6:15 KJV)

Jesus said I have not come to remove the law but to fulfill it.

Jesus gave us this Commandment;

> Jesus said unto him, Thou shalt love the Lord thy God with all thy heart, and with all thy soul, and with thy entire mind. This is the first and great commandment. And the second is like unto it, Thou shalt love thy neighbor as thyself. On these two commandments hang all the law and the prophets.
>
> Matthew 22:37-40 (KJV)

Appearing for some reason, you through religious belief continually believe the lie that you have to work to earn your way to heaven. Through that religious belief you also sometime believe God punishes you with sickness and wants you to be poor old souls that die young, loss is what God wants for His people. And you are not free until you renew your mind, and that takes a lifetime to do.

This somehow is a reword?

You toil on the outside of your home so all can see but your true needs are not taken care of thinking you have to do more, work harder and then maybe you can get a crumb. If I may, let me say this you can't work enough as to save a hair from falling off your head.

This is a gift of God it is God's grace unmerited favor.

Remember when the mother, a woman of Canaan, she came to Jesus and worshiped Him asked Him for help. Her daughter was grievously vexed with a devil, and Jesus answered and said:

> It is not meet to take the children's bread, and to cast it to dogs. And she said, Truth, Lord: yet the dogs eat of the crumbs which fall from their masters' table. Then look at what Jesus said, O woman, great is thy faith: be it unto thee even as thou wilt. And her daughter was made whole from that very hour.
>
> Matthew 15:26-28 (KJV)

What moved Jesus? It was her faith and did Jesus just give her a crumb? No way, He did what she asked Him. He took care of what was needed and her daughter was made whole.

Your personal Faith in God will always move The Hand of God regardless of what the need is. No matter how impossible it may seem to be, beyond ever being a fulfillment. It is always your faith that moves The Hand of God, when you know His word, you have a promise to hold on to, a word He has given you. He is the one that makes it happen, it is His power that does the work, all you need to do is believe and have Faith in God. It is not what you do but who you have your faith in. Whatever need you have, you have so very many scriptures to hold on to and not be moved. Get your personal word from God and hold on to it and do not let the enemy take it, keep on keeping on. Look at it as often as needed, read it over and over.

> For in Jesus Christ neither circumcision availed anything, nor uncircumcision; but faith which works by love. In James it says, what doth it profit, my brethren, though a man say he hath faith, and have not works? Can faith save him? If a brother or sister be naked, and destitute of daily food, And one of you say unto them, Depart in peace, be ye warmed and filled; notwithstanding ye give them not those things which are needful to the body; what doth it profit?
>
> (James2:14-16 KJV)

We have taken that to mean you have to work your way to heaven. Not so. James is talking to Christian believers and saying; you say you have faith and yet your brother is hungry or out in the cold, you might say it like this; your thoughts are on yourself and your own needs not others, that goes for all Christians, even Christians that are in need, if you are without, hungry and cold and look to others and say in your heart why are they not helping me? The Bible says to help me. You may even start to judge them. You are not able to walk in love with that kind of thinking. Then Satan steals the love and faith through love you need to get you over and up. You then are not looking to The Father who loves all of us and to the faith in God and His word. You cannot walk in Faith and not have love. Love for the body is our works.

Your works are the love shown to others. One is a Christian walk, the walk of Faith through love; the other is the Gift of God. The free Gift through believing in Christ all you have to do to be in Christ, a new creature in Christ, washed free, to have all the benefits of the cross and resurrection, is to Believe. "And hope makes us not ashamed; because the love of God is shed abroad in our hearts by the Holy Ghost which is given unto us". (Romans 5:5 KJV) So then God's love is in our hearts by the Holy Spirit, God even provides the love we need.

"Nor height, nor depth, nor any other creature, shall be able to separate us from the love of God, which is in Christ Jesus our Lord." (Romans 8:39 KJV) When you are in Christ not one thing can separate you from God's love. Think about this when you were still in sin before the blood of Jesus, God so loved you He sent His Son.

"Herein is love, not that we loved God, but that he loved us, and sent his Son to be the propitiation for our sins." (1 John 4:10 KJV)

"For God so loved the world, that he gave his only begotten Son, that whosoever believeth in him should not perish, but have everlasting life." (John 3:16 KJV)

"And to know the love of Christ, which passes knowledge, that ye might be filled with all the fullness of God." (Ephesians 3:19 KJV) God gives us the ability to love one another and to walk in the fullness of God's love.

"That their hearts might be comforted, being knit together in love, and unto all riches of the full assurance of understanding, to the acknowledgement of the mystery of God, and of the Father, and of Christ" (Colossians 2:2 KJV)

"Remembering without ceasing your work of faith, and labor of love, and patience of hope in our Lord Jesus Christ, in the sight of God and our Father;" (1 Thessalonians 1:3 KJV)

What then are you to do? Your work is to comfort one another, to lift up, cheer on one another, sing Psalms, Praise God, give thanks be to God for all His benefits. If a brother or sister is having a rough time you are to build them up not condemn them or wine with them, that only pulls you and them down even lower than they were to begin with. You are to be knit together in love. Walking in full assurance of this mystery of God and unto all the riches provided. Remembering without ceasing your work of faith, and labor of love, expect, hope in Our Lord Jesus Christ, in the sight of God and our Father.

"Now I beseech you, brethren, by the name of our Lord Jesus Christ, that ye all speak the same thing and that there be no divisions among you; but that ye be perfectly joined together in the same mind and in the same judgment." (1 Corinthians 1:10 KJV)

We are all one body in Christ and Christ being the head. Just as you have one God. The Father, The Son and The Holy Spirit, you are all part of Christ's body.

"For as we have many members in one body, and all members have not the same office: So we, being many, are one body in Christ, and every one members one of another." (Romans 12:4-5 KJV)

Therefore, if one of our members is in need, it affects the whole body. That is when you need to be moved with compassion as Jesus, to reach out in love, not closing our eyes or thinking someone else can take care of this.

"For as the body is one, and hath many members, and all the members of that one body, being many, are one body: so also is Christ. But now hath God set the members every one of them in the body, as it hath pleased Him. And if they were all one member, where were the body? But now are they many members, yet but one body." (1Corn.12: 17-20 ᴋᴊᴠ)

Many spend more time thinking on what "part" you are in the body, than realizing and understanding; you are the body of Christ. Thinking you have to do all this work to get God's approval. What does the word say; it is better to obey than to sacrifice. God wants obedience to His word, He is not going to count up the number of works you have done but He will know if you took time to stop and seek Him, listen to His word and obey. That is just what the enemy wants you to do, he wants you to toil, and he wants to keep the truth away from you. The truth or understanding of who you are in Christ what you have in Christ what the Father has given you who believe and are in Christ and Christ in you the hope of Glory.

My dear friends, think about this: You are the body, you are in Christ, and you, together with your brothers and sisters in Christ, make up His body. You are one body in Christ.

Glory!!!!!

Your walk as a child of God, a born again believer, a new creature in Christ Jesus, a chosen generation, a royal priesthood, an holy nation, a peculiar people; is to walk in Love in Christ.

One day as I was reading from the Love confessions by KCM Kenneth Copland Ministry, I asked Jesus; out of all that we just read, what one do you like the best? This may sound like a strange to you, to ask Jesus, but it is just part of our relationship and communication or dialogue. He gave me this on 06/21/2012.

> If ye abide in me, and my words abide in you, ye shall ask what ye will, and it shall be done unto you. Herein is my Father glorified, that ye bear much fruit; so shall ye be my disciples. As the Father hath loved me, so have I loved you: continue ye in my love. If ye keep my commandments, ye shall abide in my love; even as I have kept my Father's commandments, and abide in his love. These things have I spoken unto you, that my joy might remain in you, and that your joy might be full. This is my commandment, that ye love one another, as I have loved you. Greater love hath no man than this, that a man lay down his life for his friends.
>
> John 15:7-13 (KJV)

Glory to God, as I was just reading over what was written so far, I read in Chapter Four, where Jesus brought this word to me when I was going through a very rough time. His word was in my heart so it was able to rise up in me and comfort and bring joy and lift me up and over to victory. Now I also see why He wanted to add this, I was wondering, asking Jesus in my heart why put this in the book? Thinking this was just He and I talking.

This was the word He gave me back in June 2012. Glory! This shows you just how alive his word is. He placed it in my heart, and when I needed comfort and needed to be comforted, the Word of God rose up on the inside of me and lifted me up. There is not one thing He doesn't care about no matter how big or small.

I truly believe the Love of God is reaching out to each one wanting to be a part of your everyday life. He added this in so He, Jesus, could show you how the word works in our heart. His word comes up out of your heart to bring health and healing and strength in time of need. That is why you have to get the Word of God in you each and every day, not just on Sunday or to give Him only ten min. of your day. The greatest love you will ever know is right there every moment of every day. It does not matter what time of day or night you reach out to Him, He is always there. Think about it, every time all day all night He is there for you.

Thank You My Lord.

Chapter 8

COVENANT LIFE AND BLESSING

The Blessing; God spelled it out very clearly in Deuteronomy 28, The Blessing Jesus also spelled it out clearly in John 10; the entire wonderful Gift we have in this Blessing. In actuality the Word, The Bible, is jammed packed with blessings. God's word, the words He gives to us, provides us ALL we ever need. If you were to only receive one word from God, that one word placed in your heart by the hand of Jesus will get you through any need, any situation you would ever come up against, one revelation of one word, can and will move mountains, but only you can receive that revelation.

Let's take a close look at what God and Jesus are saying; Please pay close attention. I pray you read this with the understanding of your heart.

God said "And it shall come to pass, if thou shalt hearken diligently unto the voice of the Lord thy God, to observe and to do all his commandments which I command thee this day, that the Lord thy God will set thee on high above all nations of the earth:" (Deuteronomy 28 :1 KJV)

Jesus said "Verily, verily, I say unto you, He that entereth not by the door into the sheepfold, but climbeth up some other way, the same is a thief and a robber. But he that entereth in by the door is the shepherd of the sheep. 3 To him the porter openeth; and the sheep hear his voice: and he calleth his own sheep by name, and leadeth them out." (John 10:1-2 KJV)

God said "And all these blessings shall come on thee, and overtake thee, if thou shalt hearken unto the voice of the Lord thy God. 14 And thou shalt not go aside from any of the words which I command thee this day, to the right hand, or to the left, to go after other gods to serve them." (Deuteronomy 28:2 and 14 KJV)

Jesus said " And a stranger will they not follow, but will flee from him: for they know not the voice of strangers." (John 10:5 KJV)

God said "Blessed shalt thou be when thou comest in, and blessed shalt thou be when thou goest out. And the Lord shall make thee the head, and not the tail; and thou shalt be above only, and thou shalt not be beneath; if that thou hearken unto the commandments of the Lord thy

God, which I command thee this day, to observe and to do them:" (Deuteronomy 28:6 and 13 KJV)

Jesus said "I am the door: by me if any man enter in, he shall be saved, and shall go in and out, and find pasture. The thief cometh not, but for to steal, and to kill, and to destroy: I am come that they might have life, and that they might have it more abundantly. Jesus said; And other sheep I have, which are not of this fold: them also I must bring, and they shall hear my voice; and there shall be one fold, and one shepherd." (John 10:9, 10 and 16 KJV)

God said "And thou shalt not go aside from any of the words which I command thee this day, to the right hand, or to the left, to go after other gods to serve them. (Deuteronomy 28 :14 KJV)

Jesus said "But he that is an hireling, and not the shepherd, whose own the sheep are not, seeth the wolf coming, and leaveth the sheep, and fleeth: and the wolf catcheth them, and scattereth the sheep. The hireling fleeth, because he is an hireling, and careth not for the sheep. I am the good shepherd, and know my sheep, and am known of mine." (John 10:12-14 KJV)

God said "The Lord shall open unto thee his good treasure, the heaven to give the rain unto thy land in his season, and to bless all the work of thine hand: and thou shalt lend unto many nations, and thou shalt not borrow." (Deuteronomy 28 :12 KJV)

Jesus said " My sheep hear my voice, and I know them, and they follow me: And I give unto them eternal life; and they shall never perish, neither shall any man pluck them out of my hand. "(John 10:27-28 KJV)

Talk about a covenant. My heart is rushing out with thanksgiving and awe. What love! There is not one thing that is "Good" that God would keep from us. My heart is so full I am speechless.

So I ask You, Lord Jesus, what would "You" want to add or want to say about this Covenant we have in You?

I just got the reply and started to type and began to laugh because this is so Jesus His reply was a question.

Do you hear my voice?

> Jesus answered them, I told you, and ye believed not: the works that I do in my Father's name, they bear witness of me. But ye believe not, because ye are not of my sheep, as I said unto you.My sheep hear my voice, and I know them, and they follow me:And I give unto them eternal life; and they shall never perish, neither shall any man pluck them out of my hand.My Father, which gave them me, is greater than all; and no man is able to pluck them out of my Father's hand. I and my Father are one
>
> (John10:25-30 KJV)

Glory what an Awesome God.
Jesus gives you "The invitation."
Do you hear my voice?
Turn to page 173.
Take a moment and we will pray.

Chapter 9

TO BE BORN AGAIN

Lord Jesus You said "we must be Born Again" will You explain? "Jesus answered and said unto him, Verily, verily, I say unto thee, Except a man be born again, he cannot see the kingdom of God." (John3:3 KJV)

There was a man of the Pharisees, named Nicodemus, a ruler of the Jews:

> The same came to Jesus by night, and said unto him, Rabbi, we know that thou art a teacher come from God: for no man can do these miracles that thou doest, except God be with him. Jesus answered and said unto him, Verily, verily, I say unto thee, Except a man be born again, he cannot see the kingdom of God. Nicodemus saith unto him, How can a man be born when he is old? can he enter the second time into his mother's womb, and be born? Jesus answered, Verily, verily, I say unto thee, Except a man be born of water and of the Spirit, he cannot

enter into the kingdom of God. That which is born of the flesh is flesh; and that which is born of the Spirit is spirit.

(John3:2-6 KJV)

Jesus, for a long time I read over this and thought that Nicodemus asked you a question first, but he didn't. Your reply was from the statement his heart through his actions made. As you, so often do as shown in the word, you read the thoughts and heart, of a man. You behold and Love us.

Nicodemus was a Pharisee, a ruler of Jews, yet he came out by night to see Jesus, and said unto him, expressing the beliefs of others along with his own using the word we,

"Rabbi, we know that thou art a teacher come from God: for no man can do these miracles that thou doest, except God be with him." Except God be with Him!!! Yet when told of Jesus he must be born again he had no clue. Why by night so as that the others would not see?

"Jesus answered and said unto him, Art thou a master of Israel, and knowest not these things? Verily, verily, I say unto thee, We speak that we do know, and testify that we have seen; and ye receive not our witness." (John 3:10-11 KJV)

Nicodemus asked Jesus How, Nicodemus saith unto him, how can a man be born when he is old? Can he enter the second time into his mother's womb, and be born?Jesus says without hesitation Jesus answered, Verily, verily, I say unto thee, Except a man be born of water and of the Spirit, he cannot

enter into the kingdom of God. That which is born
of the flesh is flesh; and that which is born of the
Spirit is spirit.

(John 3:5-6 KJV)

I can recall clearly the very night I was asked the
question. Are you born again? I thought wow that's new I
had not, at that time, ever heard that term "Born Again".
I then said "I am not sure what you are asking me?" I was
asked another time are you born again, this time they did
not wait for an answer. I was then asked would you like to
receive Jesus? He will live in your heart; you are then a new
creature born over into the Kingdom of God.

Did you know just about a thousand thoughts can run
through your mind in a moments time, or it seemed as
so. I quickly ran these thoughts through; I thought I had
Jesus, at my first Communion? Because of my teaching
as a catholic, I thought ok this is a catholic charismatic
meeting I should be safe, not knowing the full knowledge
of the word and the Spirit, I didn't really know about the
born again stuff, but I said "OK God if this is from You
I want it." That was my extent of understanding to be
"Born Again".

Then real truth came through the Holy Spirit and
teaching of the word, then I had Christ in me The Holy
Sprite to guide me in the word and truths. I do believe it
is helpful if you better understand them. Not taking from
FAITH, when you are born again you actually receive

Christ; you actually are a new creature. You are now in Christ a part of His body and He in you, the hope of Glory.

You receive so very much, at the very moment you accept Christ Jesus. Let's take a closer look at being born again and some of what you receive, some of the benefits you as a child of God receive. That unmerited favor that Grace and Glory God gives you freely through the blood of His dear Son.

Lord what would You, say from Your Word that puts heavenly Wisdom into our understanding of "To Be Born Again"?

In Isaiah 1: 1-31 you pretty much read the state of mankind without accepting Jesus as Savior, you also see what the Lord God thinks of this and what He wants and will and has done;

> To what purpose is the multitude of your sacrifices unto me? saith the Lord: I am full of the burnt offerings of rams, and the fat of fed beasts; and I delight not in the blood of bullocks, or of lambs, or of he goats. When ye come to appear before me, who hath required this at your hand, to tread my courts Bring no more vain oblations; incense is an abomination unto me; the new moons and Sabbaths, the calling of assemblies, I cannot away with; it is iniquity, even the solemn meeting. Your new moons and your appointed feasts my soul hateth: they are a trouble unto me; I am weary to bear them. And when ye spread forth your hands,

I will hide mine eyes from you: yea, when ye make many prayers, I will not hear: your hands are full of blood. Wash you, make you clean; put away the evil of your doings from before mine eyes; cease to do evil;

(Isaiah 1: 11-16 KJV)

God Himself is telling us, you sin, and then go in and ask for forgiveness over and over; not repenting through the blood of Jesus it is just words that say nothing just babbling. Without Jesus you ask God to forgive you and try to make deals with God to never do this or that, but without the born again life of Jesus and the Holy Spirit, without the Blood and the power, God's power that comes with believing in Christ, you can't keep the deal you made or the vow. Nothing you do can ever clean you. But …….

"Come now, and let us reason together, saith the Lord: though your sins be as scarlet, they shall be as white as snow; though they be red like crimson, they shall be as wool.19 If ye be willing and obedient, ye shall eat the good of the land:" (Isaiah 1: 18 KJV)

Therefore said the Lord, the Lord of hosts, the mighty One of Israel, Ah, I will ease me of mine adversaries, and avenge me of mine enemies: And I will turn my hand upon thee, and purely purge away thy dross, and take away all thy tin: And I will restore thy judges as at the first, and thy counselors as at the beginning: afterward thou shalt be called,

The city of righteousness, the faithful city. Zion shall be redeemed with judgment, and her converts with righteousness.

(Isaiah 1: 24-27 KJV)

Thank You Jesus, for being obedient to the Father on my behalf. Because of You, I have eternal life and all the Promises of The Father. Because of You, I have the Father's Love.

It is the Lord that will work His plan in you, when you are in Christ.

It is the Lord that did the cleaning and purely purges, He only asks you to believe in HIM. Only He can lift you up to Glory.

Thank you Lord God Almighty, Glory to God!!!

I waited patiently for the Lord; and he inclined unto me, and heard my cry. He brought me up also out of an horrible pit, out of the miry clay, and set my feet upon a rock, and established my goings. And he hath put a new song in my mouth, even praise unto our God: many shall see it, and fear, and shall trust in the Lord. Blessed is that man that maketh the Lord his trust, and respecteth not the proud, nor such as turn aside to lies. Many, O Lord my God, are thy wonderful works which thou hast done, and thy thoughts which are to us-ward: they cannot be reckoned up in order unto thee: if I would declare and speak of them, they are more than can be numbered. Sacrifice and offering thou didst not desire; mine ears hast thou opened: burnt offering and sin offering hast thou not required.

(Psalm 40: 1-6 KJV)

To be Born Again is the only way;

Now we know that what things so ever the law saith, it saith to them who are under the law: that every mouth may be stopped, and all the world may become guilty before God. Therefore by the deeds of the law there shall no flesh be justified in his sight: for by the law is the knowledge of sin. But now the righteousness of God without the law is manifested, being witnessed by the law and the prophets; Even the righteousness of God which is by faith of Jesus Christ unto all and upon all them that believe: for there is no difference: For all have sinned, and come short of the glory of God; Being justified freely by his grace through the redemption that is in Christ Jesus: Whom God hath set forth to be a propitiation through faith in his blood, to declare his righteousness for the remission of sins that are past, through the forbearance of God

(Romans 3: 19-25 KJV)

But to him that worketh not, but believeth on him that justifieth the ungodly, his faith is counted for righteousness. Even as David also describeth the blessedness of the man, unto whom God imputeth righteousness without works, Saying, Blessed are they whose iniquities are forgiven, and whose sins are covered. Blessed is the man to whom the Lord will not impute sin. Cometh this blessedness then upon the circumcision only, or upon the uncircumcision also? for we say that faith was reckoned to Abraham for righteousness. How was it then reckoned? when he was in circumcision, or in uncircumcision? Not in circumcision, but in uncircumcision.

(Romans 4:5-10 KJV)

It is in Believing Jesus is the Christ, The Son of the Living God, who through the power of the Glory of God raised Christ Jesus.

Jesus actually died in my place and your place. He went to the lowest part of hell and carried all of our sins; all of mankind's and died in our stead. Through faith in His Father God, the Power of The Holy Spirit, He, Jesus became the first born of the Father.

"For whom he did foreknow, he also did predestinate to be conformed to the image of his Son, that he might be the firstborn among many brethren." (Romans 8:29 KJV)

I am one of many brethren from the firstborn. Are you?

When you accept Christ, the old you dies, you were buried with Christ, and Glory you are Born Again new. All things passed in that death; the old you in no longer. You are also raised with Him, Jesus, and sitting in heavenly places with Christ. The old man is what Satan wants to throw up, regurgitate in your face. But he is no more; he does not exist only in your mind if you believe Satan's lies. God does not see you that way He sees the blood of Jesus when He looks at you, you are in Christ you make up His body so you are not that old man. You are a new creature in Christ. Know this truth.

> Giving thanks unto the Father, which hath made us meet (able) to be partakers of the inheritance of the saints in light Who hath delivered us from the power of darkness, and hath translated us into the kingdom of his dear Son: In whom we have redemption through his blood, even the forgiveness of sins: Who is the image of the invisible God, the firstborn of every creature: For by him were all things created, that are in heaven, and that are in earth, visible and invisible, whether they be thrones, or dominions, or principalities, or powers: all things were created by him, and for him: And he is before all things, and by him all things consist. And he is the head of the body, the church: who is the beginning, the firstborn from the dead; that in all things he might have the preeminence. For it pleased the Father that in him should all fullness dwell;And, having made peace through the blood of his cross, by him to reconcile all things unto himself; by him, I say, whether they be things in earth, or things in heaven. And you, that were sometime alienated and enemies in your mind by wicked works, yet now hath he reconciled In the body of his flesh through death, to present

you holy and unblameable and unreproveable in his sight:

(Colossians 1: 12-22)

So when you believe God and accept Jesus as your Lord and Savior, your sin man dies that very moment, all power of death over you is gone, you are born again in Christ Jesus. You receive your benefits, you are of God, and have through Jesus become reconciled to God and given the ministry of reconciliation, with all things being of God, your benefits that only come when you are in Christ Jesus.

> Therefore if any man be in Christ, he is a new creature: old things are passed away; behold, all things are become new. And all things are of God, who hath reconciled us to himself by Jesus Christ, and hath given to us the ministry of reconciliation; To wit, that God was in Christ, reconciling the world unto himself, not imputing their trespasses unto them; and hath committed unto us the word of reconciliation.

(2Corn.5:17-19 KJV)

Only by the Blood of Jesus

> But with the precious blood of Christ, as of a lamb without blemish and without spot: Who verily was foreordained before the foundation of the world, but was manifest in these last times for you, Who by him do believe in God that raised him up from the dead, and gave him glory; that your faith and

hope might be in God. Seeing ye have purified your souls in obeying the truth through the Spirit unto unfeigned love of the brethren, see that ye love one another with a pure heart fervently: Being born again, not of corruptible seed, but of incorruptible, by the word of God, which liveth and abideth forever. For all flesh is as grass, and all the glory of man as the flower of grass. The grass withereth, and the flower thereof falleth away: But the word of the Lord endureth forever. And this is the word which by the gospel is preached unto you.

(1 Peter 1: 19-25 KJV)

Let us not walk as though we are still in the dark, let us put on the new man that you are in Christ Jesus. Truly believe in the word of God, you can, with the eyes of your spirit, see you are no longer;

Sin = to death and fear. You are righteous = to life and faith

We are a new creature born of the seed of God through Christ Jesus. We are the redeemed of Christ Christ hath redeemed us from the curse of the law, being made a curse for us: for it is written, Cursed is every one that hangeth on a tree: That the blessing of Abraham might come on the Gentiles through Jesus Christ; that we might receive the promise of the Spirit through faith.

(Galatians 3:13-14 KJV)

If you are Christ's you are Abraham seed and you are GOD'S

"Seeing ye have purified your souls in obeying the truth through the Spirit unto unfeigned love of the brethren, see that ye love one another with a pure heart fervently:" (1 Peter 1:22 KJV)

Obeying the truth and that believes on the Lord God.

> But what saith it? The word is nigh thee, even in thy mouth, and in thy heart: that is, the word of faith, which we preach; That if thou shalt confess with thy mouth the Lord Jesus, and shalt believe in thane heart that God hath raised him from the dead, thou shalt be saved. For with the heart man believeth unto righteousness; and with the mouth confession is made unto salvation. For the scripture said, whosoever believeth on him shall not be ashamed. For there is no difference between the Jew and the Greek: for the same Lord over all is rich unto all that call upon him. For whosoever shall call upon the name of the Lord shall be saved.
>
> (Romans 10:8-13 KJV)

Glory be to God!

This brings us right back to the why of things, that is, God Loves us, He, First loved us.

> That whosoever believeth in him should not perish, but have eternal life. For God so loved the world that he gave his only begotten Son, that whosoever

A Man-God Named Jesus

believeth in him should not perish, but have everlasting life. For God sent not his Son into the world to condemn the world; but that the world through him might be saved. He that believeth on him is not condemned: but he that believeth not is condemned already, because he hath not believed in the name of the only begotten Son of God.

(John 3:15-18 KJV)

In Christ, you and I are the body of Christ, and you and I are in The Kingdom of God, NOW!!!

"For the kingdom of God is not meat and drink; but righteousness, and peace, and joy in the Holy Ghost." (Romans 14: 17 KJV)

"For the kingdom of God is not in word, but in power." (1 Corinthians 4: 20 KJV)

"Now this I say, brethren, that flesh and blood cannot inherit the kingdom of God; neither doth corruption inherit incorruption." (1 Corinthians 15: 50)

We as believers have so very much, that God; Our Father in Jesus Christ through the power of The Holy Spirit has given us. Books can never contain all you have in the Kingdom of God or what God has in store for His children. Jesus did so very much for all of us. John said the world could not contain all that Jesus did while He was on earth. 25 And there are also many other things which Jesus did, the which, if they should be written every one,

135

I suppose that even the world itself could not contain the books that should be written. Amen. John 25

One day as I was reading scripture, I read that in John so asking the Holy Spirit to please explain? What I got in my spirit was, think about it, on the cross Jesus took everything that Satan placed on man, every act of evil man would ever commit, Jesus took on Himself. Not just those of a believer but ALL, everything, all sin, all sickness, all sorrow, all death, all diseases, all darkness, every evil of every kind for man, every man ever to be on the earth over all the ages and generations, for All mankind. Each individual person is loved and known to Jesus; my face your face, the most evil deranged person, was before Him on the cross; He took your sins on Himself knowing each person each individual personally.

Think about that, not just in general but each human being's face was before Jesus, known and loved by Him and the Father. The Grace of God does not stop, sin does not trump God's Hand, God is Love His Mercy endures forever. When God created and made the heavens and the earth and its entire host, your substance "you", yet not formed, yet in God's book all of your members were written. You are also fearfully and wonderfully made. Wonderfully put together and God saw everything He made and said" it is very good." For God so loved the world He sent His only Son. The Father Loved us, even though we, were still in sin before the blood of Jesus, God so loved the world!!! He Sent.

And through Jesus

"He shall see of the travail of his soul, and shall be satisfied: by his knowledge shall my righteous servant justify many; for he shall bear their iniquities." (Isaiah 53: 11 KJV)

Jesus did this for all, even for the person who will not repent and believe…….

What you have right now as a believer and what is to come in eternal life, you have in Christ. You are still in your flesh body and are living in the world, but you are not of this world. You have your life and liberty in the unseen by Faith, which is one reason you struggle in this flesh body from the seen to the unseen. You must keep your focus with the eyes of your spirit.

Pray to know and comprehend the word of God and pray for the eyes of your understanding to be enlightened with truth. Look in the word for what God says; spend your time on believing the word of God in faith, not how He is going to do it. When Moses came to the Red Sea, I don't think he stopped and said to God, well God how you going to do this lets see we could ……

No he said; in his heart, God the I Am said He would deliver His people.

Paul prays this for the body as you also should.

That we should be to the praise of his glory, who first trusted in Christ. In whom ye also trusted, after that ye heard the word of truth, the gospel of your salvation: in whom also after that ye believed, ye were sealed with that Holy Spirit of promise, That the God of our Lord Jesus Christ, the Father of glory, may give unto you the spirit of wisdom and revelation in the knowledge of him: The eyes of your understanding being enlightened; that ye may know what is the hope of his calling, and what the riches of the glory of his inheritance in the saints,

And what is the exceeding greatness of his power to us-ward who believe, according to the working of his mighty power, Which he wrought in Christ, when he raised him from the dead, and set him at his own right hand in the heavenly places, Far above all principality, and power, and might, and dominion, and every name that is named, not only in this world, but also in that which is to come: And hath put all things under his feet, and gave him to be the head over all things to the church, Which is his body, the fulness of him that filleth all in all

(Ephesians 1: 12-23KJV)

Being born again is an individual personal walk between you and The Lord, along with a responsibility to the body of Christ that you are now a part of. Throughout the New Testament you are told to love one another and to strengthen, build up and edify one another in the Lord, to be a part of the Body of Christ. You are to love yourself and one another.

If you love and care for yourself you are going to nurture and take care of your body. Eat right get the rest you need and so on. The full care and love for oneself and others is not just the care of your physical needs but our spiritual and mental needs. Love covers the Spirit, Soul and body, Jesus shows love, the Father Shows love, the word tells you, you are to love God with all your being and to love your neighbor as yourself. Well for some of you, you may need to learn how to love and care for yourself, not in a selfish way but as God intended. Some of you have to learn how to not only love others; you also have to learn how to love yourself, Spirit, Soul and Body.

You all want that "perfect" life, so you start off on your walk with God ready to conquer all. You then try to start changing the people you live with, trying to get them to go to church with you. That is not a bad thing; but if over the past years I have learned anything, it is that the only person you need to work on or that you can change is yourself. You can show others Jesus in you and as the Lord leads, minister to them, and witnessing to others. But let's look at a trap you may find yourself in, the traps the enemy uses. I am talking about the very person that you want to bring to the Lord, the person you want to share this life with, your spouse, your kids, boyfriend or girlfriend. You know every time you go to a service, your thoughts are, man it was right on, they should have been there, I wish so in so was here they sure do need that, and you want them to be with you and so on. You want that perfect relationship, you want for it to work, for them to get it. So you can have that happy ever after.

They may even go to church a few times with you then, you may hear words like, oh why don't we stay home today or maybe, I don't like the way they look at me, and then it starts. Slowly, for one reason or another you stop going right along with them. This doesn't just have to be about going to church, it could be reading the word, getting up a little extra early, but eventually you backslide and stop seeking God yourself. You may even continue going to church, but every service you are on, you keep asking yourself why they are not there and why they can't come. So the teaching you need for your own growth is not received because your mind was on the loss or lack, not listening to the word intended for your own growth or on the blessing, which you are to receive now.

Let's use this as an example; if you have ever been on a plane, you are told before takeoff or shortly there in, if the cabin loses pressure, oxygen mask will drop down from the overhead compartment, securely fasten it over your face, if you are traveling with small children or with someone who would need help, FIRST securely fasten on your own mask then help the other person. Otherwise you both may be in need of help, and too weak to be able to help one another.

Just as someone trying to stop using drugs is not able to start out leading a person to recovery until they are securely grounded, and even when grounded, they will still have to continue on with the program.

You may even find yourself so overwhelmed trying to get everyone to go to church. You may get discouraged, trying to get them to know the dos and don'ts of being a Christian. You may even fall back and think this is not working, I can't do all this stuff, so the door to the schemes of the enemy is opened without you even knowing it.

The GOOD NEWS is not the dos and don'ts of being in Christ. It is the Love of God made flesh for all mankind. Until you have a solid foundation for yourself you will be just like the person trying to put the oxygen mask on the other person first, wanting to help your love one and without the knowledge and support of a strong foundation you fall or draw back.

When you are born again and filled with the Holy Spirit He (The Spirit) helps you examine your thoughts if we ask Him to, and to understand the ways of God by reading The Word of God. You learn Gods ways and Promises so as not to become "double minded" to ponder our steps to be established by God. Up to this point you reacted to your feelings, if you feel sad you must be sad, if you feel helpless you must be helpless. Because you feel helpless or sad does not mean you are.

Let me give you an example; you are driving to the beach, it is a beautiful day sun shining the top down on your car the ocean salt air breeze fills the air. You are feeling pretty good, out of nowhere a car cuts you off, so you turn the wheel of your car in order to not hit the car in front of you, you then drive off the road on to the pavement. No one is hurt but you are sitting in the car now pretty shook up. I trust you first thank God, but then you have a choice. You can praise God and thank Him and continue on to the beach, all of the same elements are still present, or you can start cursing the driver, going on and on about what a jerk of a driver he is, and drive on to the beach or forget going to the beach altogether. See, you have a choice to do what the word says and not take offence or let your feelings take over and act out your thoughts. Then so becoming what you feel.

Trust God not your feelings. You can use your feelings as indicators to help you make the right decision on what you are feeling. Do I need more rest? Why do I feel fearful? Feelings are wonderful tools God gave you to bring truth, care and love into your life. Providing you bring your feelings to The Lord that through the power of the Holy Spirit you will receive peace in that situation. Every time you have a feeling you need to take it to the Lord in prayer. You may say I don't feel Holy, I don't feel Born Again, or even I don't feel Righteous. When you take your feelings to the Lord in prayer you are allowing the Holy Spirit to bring truth in. Looking to the word of God, what does the word say about this? You will then find you are increasing in your relationship with the Father. You may even find that you are feeling less and less of what you bring to Him because He is working out the peace you need. And you are receiving God's peace that keeps your heart and mind in Christ Jesus.

So as you learn to care for yourself as God would want you to, you also have to learn to love the body of Christ as your own body. Not talking about one another, or looking down on or even looking as though they are above you, but to love them as Christ has loved you. To have compassion for, and compassion is an action word, Jesus always did something when He had compassion for someone. It is not sympathy for, or a feeling of hopelessness, but of love, the love of God that is able to move you on up to Glory.

You as a believer are in the Kingdom of God; it is not a magical place or a fairytale land it is where God's family lives and where you find strength and life to face each day.

> Whosoever believeth that Jesus is the Christ is born of God: and every one that loveth him that begat loveth him also that is begotten of him. By this we know that we love the children of God, when we love God, and keep his commandments. For this is the love of God, that we keep his commandments: and his commandments are not grievous. For whatsoever is born of God overcometh the world: and this is the victory that overcometh the world, even our faith. Who is he that overcometh the world, but he that believeth that Jesus is the Son of God? This is he that came by water and blood,

even Jesus Christ; not by water only, but by water and blood. And it is the Spirit that beareth witness, because the Spirit is truth. For there are three that bear record in heaven, the Father, the Word, and the Holy Ghost: and these three are one. And there are three that bear witness in earth, the Spirit, and the water, and the blood: and these three agree in one. If we receive the witness of men, the witness of God is greater: for this is the witness of God which he hath testified of his Son. He that believeth on the Son of God hath the witness in himself: he that believeth not God hath made him a liar; because he believeth not the record that God gave of his Son.

(1 John 5: 1-10 KJV)

Chapter 10

WALKING IN LOVE

Jesus You told us that the greatest commandment is this; "Jesus said unto him, Thou shalt love the Lord thy God with all thy heart, and with all thy soul, and with all thy mind. This is the first and great commandment. And the second is like unto it, Thou shalt love thy neighbor as thyself. On these two commandments hang all the law and the prophets." (Matthew 22;37-40 KJV)

To love God with every fiber of your being, to love your neighbor as yourself, that to walk in love covers all things that the law of the prophets speak.

Will you explain in your word what and how to do this and why? Please.

The word says; you are under the Grace not the Law, the Grace fulfills the Law walking in Love, Love does not remove the Low it completes it. What we could never do, in Christ we are able. By walking in His Love, God's Love is shed abroad in our hearts by the Holy Spirit. Without

Jesus, The Father, and the Holy Spirit, you are still under the Law, incomplete never able. When you are Born Again you are under the Grace and become able to walk in Love.

Look at what Jesus was saying about the Law, and taking it to a complete new level, when you walk in Love, in Christ, Christ shows how you can walk in this complete new level. The Grace, the glorious Grace Jesus provides. When you walk in love it is for your own good also, bringing peace and health to your body.

> But I say unto you which hear, Love your enemies, do good to them which hate you, Bless them that curse you, and pray for them which despitefully use you. And unto him that smiteth thee on the one cheek offer also the other; and him that taketh away thy cloak forbid not to take thy coat also. Give to every man that asketh of thee; and of him that taketh away thy goods ask them not again. And as ye would that men should do to you, do ye also to them likewise. For if ye love them which love you, what thank have ye? for sinners also love those that love them. And if ye do good to them which do good to you, what thank have ye? for sinners also do even the same. And if ye lend to them of whom ye hope to receive, what thank have ye? for sinners also lend to sinners, to receive as much again. But love ye your enemies, and do good, and lend, hoping for nothing again; and your reward shall be great, and ye shall be the children of the Highest: for he is kind

unto the unthankful and to the evil. Be ye therefore merciful, as your Father also is merciful. Judge not, and ye shall not be judged: condemn not, and ye shall not be condemned: forgive, and ye shall be forgiven: Give, and it shall be given unto you; good measure, pressed down, and shaken together, and running over, shall men give into your bosom. For with the same measure that ye mete withal it shall be measured to you again. And he spake a parable unto them, Can the blind lead the blind? shall they not both fall into the ditch? The disciple is not above his master: but every one that is perfect shall be as his master. And why beholdest thou the mote that is in thy brother's eye, but perceivest not the beam that is in thine own eye? Either how canst thou say to thy brother, Brother, let me pull out the mote that is in thine eye, when thou thyself beholdest not the beam that is in thine own eye? Thou hypocrite, cast out first the beam out of thine own eye, and then shalt thou see clearly to pull out the mote that is in thy brother's eye. For a good tree bringeth not forth corrupt fruit; neither doth a corrupt tree bring forth good fruit. For every tree is known by his own fruit. For of thorns men do not gather figs, nor of a bramble bush gather they grapes. A good man out of the good treasure of his heart bringeth forth that which is good; and an evil man out of the evil treasure of his heart bringeth forth that which is evil: for of the abundance of the heart his mouth speaketh. And why call ye me, Lord, Lord, and do not the things which I say?

(Luke 6:27-46)

Some find this hard or full of rules but it is not rules or even do's and don'ts, it is the how to have the fullness of love, when you walk in love and the Holy Spirit helps you. You find that God wants your heart He wants your love not your do this or do that. The closer you come to Him and experience His love for you, the easier it becomes to walk in His love toward others.

One day as I was praying I said to the Lord, Lord I give You control of my thoughts, my mind and as I was saying this I heard in my spirit I don't want control I want you to choose to do it, it is your heart and love I want not control of them. What He does do is help us through the Holy Spirit. Let me give you an example. When I would see my mother and the void on her face, and in her eyes and the fact that she does not know who I am, those thoughts would get in my head, so I would pray and the Spirit would help me think on good things, I could in my mind see my mother dancing like we did when I was a child, we did the twist together and then good thoughts would come to my mind. He always helps me, He never leaves me, as I keep on praying for my mother trusting and Praising Him in all things not for all things. " In everything give thanks: for this is the will of God in Christ Jesus concerning you." (1 Thessalonians 5:18 KJV)

Jesus showed me in His word that He gave us a pattern to go by or a diagram that we can follow. Jesus says exactly what He hears from the Father and tells us very plainly so that the Spirit of God if you ask, will reveal all things to you when you ask Him. Walking in His Love His Grace His Power and Authority you are able to rise up over the flesh and enter a greater Love walk.

Let's look at what Jesus was saying in Luke 6: 27-30

> But I say unto you which hear, Love your enemies, do good to them which hate you, Bless them that curse you, and pray for them which despitefully use you. And unto him that smiteth thee on the one cheek offer also the other; and him that taketh away thy cloak forbid not to take thy coat also. Give to every man that asketh of thee; and of him that taketh away thy goods ask them not again.

(Luke 6: 27-30 KJV)

These are 8 (eight) steps Jesus shows in His word;

Love your enemies, you are taught your real enemies are Satan and his workers, to look at the sin not the sinner or the one who hurt you, not to take offence, why? Being angry at them doesn't hurt them, it only hurts you, leaving bitterness and a door that the real enemy can come in and wreak all types of havoc. So praying for them brings you peace and health also your own forgiveness, and does not separate you from God in any way. Always ask yourself, is it worth all I would lose to be upset with them or anyone?

Should you, or when you do, quickly repent and ask God for His forgiveness.

Do good to them which hate you, do well to them, the greatest gift you can give anyone is your prayers in faith. Remember God wants your heart, do what you can in Christ, love the person through Christ, praying for Salvation for them to the Lord. Through Him you can. It really is for your good.

Bless them that curse you, the greatest blessing is to ask for salvation on that person. That is the greatest gift, salvation keep your thoughts on salvation of Christ for them and then you are not tempted to think on other things bringing in envy and strife to your heart. No one would want to see a person spend eternity in hell. Know that with praying for salvation for others, always brings blessing to the person who prays.

Pray for them which despitefully use you, the word despitefully is regardless of or contrary to, it might have been prevented or something is done unexpectedly. This means taking your eye off from you, and placing it on the Lord. God does not want you to be used by others, but others may do so without even knowing it. Hold that feeling up to the Lord and keep your eyes on Him. Listen to what the Holy Spirit has to say. The Lord is always faithful, He will always bless and raise you up and give you insight in each situation.

> Unto him that smiteth thee on the one cheek offer also the other, let's look at that word. The word

smiteth in Strong's Concordance has several words to look at, let's look at this; 3960 which denote a usually single blow with the hand or any instrument. 5177, an accidental collision; by implication, to punish; figuratively, to offend (the conscience):— beat, smite, strike, wound.

(Strong's Concordance)

What does the word tell us? Great peace have they which love thy law: and nothing shall offend them ." (Psalm 119:165 KJV)

Do not hold it in offence in your heart, which only hurts you. Jesus is not telling you to be a door mat and just stand and take abuse. No, if someone keeps on, do not take that and place it in your heart agents them take it to the Lord. Do what the word says and take care of yourself. Walking in love is work, this is the "works" we can do in Christ, walk in love. You may say, "But I am right. They did me wrong." And right you very well may be, but you can give up that right to the Lord. In the book of Ruth, Boaz said unto the kinsman of Naomi, to redeem the field you must also take Ruth but that was not what he wanted to do, it would mar his own inheritance. So he gave up that right to Boaz. As per custom, "Now this was the manner in former time in Israel concerning redeeming and concerning changing, for to confirm all things; a man plucked off his shoe, and gave it to his neighbor: and this was a testimony in Israel.

Therefore the kinsman said unto Boaz, Buy it for thee. So he drew off his shoe." (Ruth 4:7-8 KJV)

If you hold that offence what mar would affect you? Would it be worth it?

In the New Testament we read the place where Jesus washed the disciples and when Jesus gets to Peter, Peter says no way "Then cometh he to Simon Peter: and Peter saith unto him, Lord, dost thou wash my feet? Jesus answered and said unto him, What I do thou knowest not now; but thou shalt know hereafter. Peter saith unto him, Thou shalt never wash my feet. Jesus answered him, If I wash thee not, thou hast no part with me." (John 13:6-8 KJV)

Peter was right in saying this; a Rabbi would never wash his disciple's feet. To be in the Love walk and to do as Jesus did, Peter had to give up what he very well knew was right, but not worth the cost to be right. You also have to look at the cost of being right. So the question is, do I take off my shoe and give it over or do I keep it and lose in the end? The Spirit of God, my friend, will always reveal to you if you ask.

Him that takes away thy cloak forbid not to take thy coat also; Be always willing to give to others, never put "thing" over a person. Do not hold harm in your heart. When you give you will always receive more from God, if you do not harbor resentment. Give in Love.

The last two go along with this; Give to every man that asked of thee; and of him that takes away thy goods ask them not again.

Using the wisdom from above, give when asked always seeking God first. Really you must always ask God before you do anything. Jesus also said and of him that takes away thy goods ask them not again. You can take the blessing God would give and if you keep doing for someone you could cause that person to become dependent on you or others, not on the Lord. Or that they expect someone to give to them their needs and maybe even their wants. They could become takers and expect from others. Then you are enabling, doing for someone what they could do for them self, not helping, not hearing what the Spirit is saying.

When you walk in love, you don't have laws or rules; you just walk as the Spirit leads. Are you going to be tested by the devil? Oh yes you are, but you are not alone, when you are in Christ you have the overcoming victory ability in you.

Jesus says; that you should do as you would want others to do to you. And if you love and do good to only them that love you and are good to you what effort is that? Do you want to produce good fruit? Then, Love and do good to them that take you to your knees to the Lord in prayer. This will produce good fruit.

If this sounds hard to do, let me tell you an easy way. The more you read the word of God and bring your thoughts in line with what the word says, the easier it becomes. The easier it is to walk in Love. If you stumble, repent quickly and God will forgive you. You will find, your health will start to improve and the less you will walk in crises with fear and torment, and more in faith that brings The Glory and Great Grace on you, your family, and all that you set your hands to.

Chapter 11

THE HOLY SPIRIT

A s I pray Dear Jesus, what more do you want to talk about, sensing in my spirit, You wanted me to ask You about The Spirit. So Dear Jesus what do you want to reveal about The Spirit of God at this time?

Jesus said; "And, behold, I send the promise of my Father upon you: but tarry ye in the city of Jerusalem, until ye be endued with power from on high." (Luke 24:49 KJV)

"But the Comforter, which is the Holy Ghost, whom the Father will send in my name, he shall teach you all things, and bring all things to your remembrance, whatsoever I have said unto you. (John 14:26 KJV)

But when the Comforter is come, whom I will send unto you from the Father, even the Spirit of truth, which proceedeth from the Father, he shall testify of me:" (John 15:26 KJV)

Nevertheless I tell you the truth; It is expedient for you that I go away: for if I go not away, the Comforter will not come unto you; but if I depart, I will send him unto you. And when he is come, he will reprove the world of sin, and of righteousness, and of judgment: Of sin, because they believe not on me; Of righteousness, because I go to my Father, and ye see me no more; Of judgment, because the prince of this world is judged. I have yet many things to say unto you, but ye cannot bear them now. Howbeit when he, the Spirit of truth, is come, he will guide you into all truth: for he shall not speak of himself; but whatsoever he shall hear, that shall he speak: and he will shew you things to come. He shall glorify me: for he shall receive of mine, and shall shew it unto you. All things that the Father hath are mine: therefore said I, that he shall take of mine, and shall shew it unto you."

(John 16:7-15 KJV)

"And hope maketh not ashamed; because the love of God is shed abroad in our hearts by the Holy Ghost which is given unto us." (Romans 5:5 KJV)

"Wherefore I put thee in remembrance that thou stir up the gift of God, which is in thee by the putting on of my hands. For God hath not given us the spirit of fear; but of power, and of love, and of a sound mind." (2 Timothy 1:6-7KJV)

"No man hath seen God at any time. If we love one another, God dwelleth in us, and his love is perfected in us. Hereby know we that we dwell in him, and he in us, because he hath given us of his Spirit." (1 John 4: 12-13 KJV)

> For the Son of God, Jesus Christ, who was preached among you by us, even by me and Silvanus and Timotheus, was not yea and nay, but in him was yea. For all the promises of God in him are yea, and in him Amen, unto the glory of God by us. Now he which stablisheth us with you in Christ, and hath anointed us, is God; Who hath also sealed us, and given the earnest of the Spirit in our hearts.
>
> (2 Corinthians 1:19-22 KJV)

To cover just some of what the Holy Spirit is, would be a book in itself. He is The Spirit of God, Power, Glory, Truth, your helper, your connection to God. He is The Third Person of the Trinity God and through the Holy Spirit you are in Christ and one with God.

Every day I take time throughout my day to pray in the Spirit, 6am 9am 12noon 3pm 7:30pm I set my phone to alert me at that time, then I pray in the Spirit. That is not the only time I pray but it is just something I do, and has been very helpful to me.

In the mornings I pray as the Spirit leads for my family as He reveals, I pray a protection around my children and grandchildren for generations to come till Jesus come. For my husband, my mother, our family, and myself, our

Leaders and for the Nations. I have always said and still say each day; "Lord, You go before me, You are always at my right side and Your Glory, The Glory of You Lord, is my rear guard. I pray with God's permission that His Angels go before us, beside us, and all around us, all the places the soles of our feet will go, prepare the goings in and out, keeping all evil, misfortune and calamity far from us all. And God's Glory keeps us." I pray as The Spirit leads and I pray in the Spirit.

I am saying this to bring you to a testimony of one manifestation of how the Spirit is so powerful and full of Glory.

In August of 2012 I was on my way back home from picking up my grandson from a friend's house after school. I had just gotten off work. It was about 6: p.m.. We were driving down the road when all of a sudden I saw a red truck going in to the turning median lane. He kept turning, right in front of our truck, (by the way I didn't usually take the truck. Up to this point I had always taken the car because it had the parking sticker, but thanks to the Holy Spirit, the night before I said to my husband, " I think I will take the truck to work in the morning." So I drove the truck, thank you Lord God, thank You, that I did drive the truck.) We were going about 30 + miles per hour, and the driver of the red truck just kept coming. I put my breaks on and tried to turn right to keep out of the way, and saying to the Lord "Lord Jesus he is not stopping, we need your help." While reaching over across to my grandson. Well, we hit and we hit hard. The air bags deployed. Things that were in the back came to the front. Smoke filled the truck and the sound of the crash still ringing in my ears, the horn just a blaring. I quickly looked over to my grandson to see how he was. Saying to him we need to get out of the truck, he, by the grace of God, opened the passenger door that later we were unable to move or open. He was fine and so was I. The crash totaled our F 150 and it was not a small truck. My grandson and I were a little shook up to say the least, but we were ok. The driver of the red truck was brought to the hospital; he had been drinking and driving on a suspended license. I was so thankful to the Lord that my grandson was fine!!!! The next day I was sitting and talking with my husband and going over with him what had taken place. As I did, I was picturing the crash in my mind, when the Lord revealed what I saw just before impact. White all white, all I saw was white, like being surrounded in all white my grandson and myself, then I heard in my spirit that was the Glory of God! The Glory of the Lord protected you and your grandson. This still brings tears and over flowing love in my heart. Thank you my God, Your Awesome Power of Your Spirit, Your Glory.

What an awesome God!!!

People, The Holy Spirit is so important to know to grow in the Lord. He is the third person of the Trinity; He is a Person of The God head. Thank God the Father for sending us His Spirit.

> Lord I Pray For this cause we (I) also, since the day we heard it, do not cease to pray for you, and to desire that ye (we) might be filled with the knowledge of his will in all wisdom and spiritual understanding; That ye (we) might walk worthy of the Lord unto all pleasing, being fruitful in every good work, and increasing in the knowledge of God; (That we are) Strengthened with all might, according to his glorious power, unto all patience and longsuffering (Expectancy not giving up) with joyfulness; (That we) Giving thanks unto the Father, which hath made us meet (able) to be partakers of the inheritance of the saints in light: Who hath delivered us from the power of darkness, and hath translated us into the kingdom of his dear Son: In whom we have redemption through his blood, even the forgiveness of sins: Who is the image of the invisible God, the firstborn of every creature:
>
> (Colossians 1:9-15 KJV)

That we Lord are your lucious fruit, that in Christ we thrive with nourishment, in Your Grace Your Glory and the abundance of Your love, that drips and over flows in the Holy Spirit. Amen

Chapter 12

I THIRST

L ord Jesus Your word says our focus is to keep our eyes on the Victory, keeping our faith on the author and finisher of our faith. In Hebrews we read "Looking unto Jesus the author and finisher of our faith; who for the joy that was set before him endured the cross, despising the shame, and is set down at the right hand of the throne of God." (Hebrews 12: 2 KJV)

Jesus, You are our Author, the Greek word meaning a chief leader, beginning, first and finisher, the Greek word meaning completer or last) of our faith. We are to keep looking to You, Jesus, and not to the how, when, why, of things. You are the author and finisher of our faith. Our part is to just stand on Your word You give us. Lord Jesus in Your Ministry on earth, You only said what the Father said and You only did what the Father did. Lord Jesus You are the perfect example, You said to your disciples if you see me you see the Father. Looking at the Father got You through the tremendous death and Glorious Resurrection. Lord Jesus through Your cross and Resurrection Your life, You as a Man, all that You walked through, Your time on earth, You walked in total Victory, help us see how you did this, please.

Lord Jesus out of all the things, beatings beyond recognition, unbelievable cruel treatment that you endured on the way to the cross and on the cross then three days in the lowest pit, You never took your eyes off the Father. Knowing the joy that was set before you, despising the shame, You sat down at the right hand of the throne of God. I can say You literally went through Hell; and Glory raised you Up!!!!

Lord Jesus, what stands out in my mind when I read the word of Your death and resurrection, all that You went through you said but few words Jesus, just before Your death and resurrection, Lord, through Your Holy Spirit please reveal what You are saying.

> After this, Jesus knowing that all things were now accomplished, that the scripture might be fulfilled, saith, "I thirst." Now there was set a vessel full of vinegar: and they filled a sponge with vinegar, and put it upon hyssop, and put it to his mouth. When Jesus therefore had received the vinegar, he said, It is finished: and he bowed his head, and gave up the ghost.
>
> (John 19:28-30 KJV)

I thirst, what did that mean I thirst? Jesus, You were beaten, whipped, spit on, all manner of torture and yet You make the statement "I thirst"?

I have pondered the fact that You said "I thirst", Lord, why I thirst?

In my spirit, I received, that was when Jesus Himself took up on Himself all sin and death of mankind. It was not the thirst to drink for the body but the extreme dryness apart from the living water. He had all mankind's sins, our grief's, our sorrows, our transgressions, our iniquities, our chastisement of our peace and took it all for our healing in every area of our life.

He was separate from God His Father for us. Jesus felt the pain of separation from God.

He Himself was the first to repent for mankind, when He said "I thirst".

He was speaking repentance. His whole life pointed to The Father in saying I Thirst He was calling to God with His last breath the Word! Glory.

The Lord said when you read my word, read it in LOVE all that the Father is, is love. His entire life Jesus spoke the way for us to see His Father. Our walk is to walk with our eyes on the word as Jesus did. Jesus knew the Word, The Good News, His Gospel, the way of salvation.

"I stretch forth my hands unto thee: my soul thirsteth after thee, as a thirsty land. Selah." And He said, "I thirst." "Hear me speedily, O LORD: my spirit faileth: hide not thy face from me, lest I be like unto them that go down into the pit." (Psalm 143:6-7 KJV) And He said, "I thirst."

"My soul thirsteth for God, for the living God: when shall I come and appear before God? My tears have been my meat day and night, while they continually say unto me, Where is thy God?" Psalm 42:2-3 KJV)

He placed all His trust, Faith in the Word. And He said, "I thirst."

"O God, thou art my God; early will I seek thee: my soul thirsteth for thee, my flesh longeth for thee in a dry and thirsty land, where no water is; To see thy power and thy glory, so as I have seen thee in the sanctuary. Because thy loving-kindness is better than life, my lips shall praise thee." (Psalm 63: 1-3 KJV)

He kept His eyes on God's power to glory. And He said, "I thirst."

"Reproach hath broken my heart; and I am full of heaviness: and I looked for some to take pity, but there was none; and for comforters, but I found none. They gave me also gall for my meat; and in my thirst they gave me vinegar to drink. Let their table become a snare before them: and that which should have been for their welfare, let it become a trap. (Psalm 69: 20-22KJV)

Jesus knew why He came, to set the captives free. The Lord said in Luke;

> The Spirit of the Lord is upon me, because he hath anointed me to preach the gospel to the poor; he

hath sent me to heal the brokenhearted, to preach deliverance to the captives, and recovering of sight to the blind, to set at liberty them that are bruised, To preach the acceptable year of the Lord. And he closed the book, and he gave it again to the minister, and sat down. And the eyes of all them that were in the synagogue were fastened on him. And he began to say unto them, This day is this scripture fulfilled in your ears.

(Luke 4:18-21 KJV)

He said, "It is Finished"; He Knew also of the Victory

"When the poor and needy seek water, and there is none, and their tongue faileth for thirst, I the LORD will hear them, I the God of Israel will not forsake them. I will open rivers in high places, and fountains in the midst of the valleys: I will make the wilderness a pool of water, and the dry land springs of water." (Isaiah 41: 17-18 KJV)

Thus saith the LORD that made thee, and formed thee from the womb, which will help thee; Fear not, O Jacob, my servant; and thou, Jesurun, whom I have chosen. For I will pour water upon him that is thirsty, and floods upon the dry ground: I will pour my spirit upon thy seed, and my blessing upon thine offspring: And they shall spring up as among the grass, as willows by the water courses. One shall say, I am the LORD's; and another shall call himself by the name of Jacob; and another shall subscribe with his hand unto the LORD, and surname himself by the name of Israel. Thus saith the LORD the King of Israel, and his redeemer the LORD of hosts; I am the first, and I am the last; and beside me there is no God.

(Isaiah 44: 2-6 KJV)

Glory to God! And He gave up the Ghosts. But His eyes never left the Father.

Jesus knew what was to come, first He knew who He was and He knew who His Father is and He knew the scriptures. His eyes never left the father or what He was called to do.

Then certain of the scribes and of the Pharisees answered, saying, Master, we would see a sign from thee. But he answered and said unto them, An evil and adulterous generation seeketh after a sign; and there shall no sign be given to it, but the sign of the prophet Jonas: For as Jonas was three days and three nights in the whale's belly; so shall the Son of man be three days and three nights in the heart of the earth.

(Matt 12: 38-40 KJV)

"Jesus answered and said unto her, Whosoever drinketh of this water shall thirst again: But whosoever drinketh of the water that I shall give him shall never thirst; but the water that I shall give him shall be in him a well of water springing up into everlasting life." (John 4: 13-14 KJV) And He said "I thirst"

"Blotting out the handwriting of ordinances that was against us, which was contrary to us, and took it out of the way, nailing it to his cross; And having spoiled principalities and powers, he made a shew of them openly, triumphing over them in it." (Colossians 2: 14-15 KJV) He said "I thirst"

His eyes never left the Fathers Thrown.

"O Lord, thou art my God; I will exalt thee, I will praise thy name; for thou hast done wonderful things; thy counsels of old are faithfulness and truth." (Isaiah 25: 1 KJV)

Jesus's eyes were always on the Father, knowing the word.

> For thou hast made of a city an heap; of a defenced city a ruin: a palace of strangers to be no city; it shall never be built. Therefore shall the strong people glorify thee, the city of the terrible nations shall fear thee. For thou hast been a strength to the poor, a strength to the needy in his distress, a refuge from the storm, a shadow from the heat, when the blast of the terrible ones is as a storm against the wall.
>
> (Isaiah 25:2-4 KJV)

Faithfull Father always Faithfull

> Thou shalt bring down the noise of strangers, as the heat in a dry place; even the heat with the shadow of a cloud: the branch of the terrible ones shall be

brought low. And in this mountain shall the LORD of hosts make unto all people a feast of fat things, a feast of wines on the lees, of fat things full of marrow, of wines on the lees well refined. And he will destroy in this mountain the face of the covering cast over all people, and the vail that is spread over all nations. He will swallow up death in victory; and the Lord GOD will wipe away tears from off all faces; and the rebuke of his people shall he take away from off all the earth: for the LORD hath spoken it. And it shall be said in that day, Lo, this is our God; we have waited for him, and he will save us: this is the LORD; we have waited for him, we will be glad and rejoice in his salvation. For in this mountain shall the hand of the LORD rest, and Moab shall be trodden down under him, even as straw is trodden down for the dunghill. And he shall spread forth his hands in the midst of them, as he that swimmeth spreadeth forth his hands to swim: and he shall bring down their pride together with the spoils of their hands. And the fortress of the high fort of thy walls shall he bring down, lay low, and bring to the ground, even to the dust.

(Isaiah 25:5-12 KJV)

His eyes never left the Fathers Thrown He knew He had Victory!!

Thus saith the LORD, In an acceptable time have I heard thee, and in a day of salvation have I helped thee: and I will preserve thee, and give thee for a covenant of the people, to establish the earth, to cause to inherit the desolate heritages; That thou mayest say to the prisoners, Go forth; to them that are in darkness, Shew yourselves. They shall feed in the ways, and their pastures shall be in all high places. They shall not hunger nor thirst; neither shall the heat nor sun smite them: for he that hath mercy on them shall lead them, even by the springs of water shall he guide them. And I will make all my mountains a way, and my highways shall be exalted. Behold, these shall come from far: and, lo, these from the north and from the west; and these from the land of Sinim. Sing, O heavens; and be joyful, O earth; and break forth into singing, O mountains: for the LORD hath comforted his people, and will have mercy upon his afflicted.

(Isaiah 49: 8-13 KJV)

He said "I thirst"

After this I beheld, and, lo, a great multitude, which no man could number, of all nations, and kindreds, and people, and tongues, stood before the throne, and before the Lamb, clothed with white robes, and palms in their hands; And cried with a loud voice, saying, Salvation to our God which sitteth upon the throne, and unto the Lamb. And all the angels stood round about the throne, and about the elders and the four beasts, and fell before the throne on their faces, and worshipped God, Saying, Amen: Blessing, and glory, and wisdom, and thanksgiving, and honor, and power, and might, be unto our God for ever and ever. Amen. And one of the elders answered, saying unto me, What are these which are arrayed in white robes? And whence came they? And I said unto him, Sir, thou knowest. And he said to me, These are they which came out of great tribulation, and have washed their robes, and made them white in the blood of the Lamb. Therefore are they before the throne of God, and serve him day and night in his temple: and he that sitteth on the throne shall dwell among them. They shall hunger no more, neither thirst anymore; neither shall the sun light on them, nor any heat. For the Lamb which is in the midst of the throne shall feed them, and shall lead them unto living fountains of waters: and God shall wipe away all tears from their eyes.

(Revelation 7: 9-17 KJV)

This picture is only a small glimpse of what is to come but Jesus knows, Jesus had His faith on heaven's throne where the Father is. Where He is.

Jesus is the perfect example for us all to follow. When the enemy starts his junk, sometimes before you even realize it, it is overwhelming, "stop" look to Jesus, you have The Holy Spirit you have Jesus, who already overcame all things for you, look to Him, He gives you His word, to help get you through all you would ever have to come up against.

Following His example, He kept His eyes on the Father and the word all the time, all the way to total Victory.

No matter what you walk in or go through as long as you are in Christ you have the Total Victory. Jesus paid the price in full. I am not saying it is always a walk in the park, which is why the word is so very important to put in your heart. We all have times when things may become overwhelming, that circumstances seem to get to you. Times when you may need the body of Christ, to reach out to for comfort or to comfort others. You have not been made islands to yourself, but one Body in Him tightly knit together in love. You need others in fellowship and communication one to another. Knowing the word and walking in love and faith in God, you have the help to rise you up.

Go to the word of God, find your own scripture to get you into your place of victory in Christ. So you can stand on God's word and not be moved no matter what comes at you. You are then rooted and built up in Him, established in faith, as you have been taught, abounding therein with thanksgiving and praise to the Father.

Jesus is our High Priest the Veil was torn. We can now go in the Holy of Holy's through the Blood of the Lamb. You and I are cleansed from all unrighteousness. We are more than conquerors in Christ Jesus. We can walk in victory; He will never leave us or forsake us. He Loves us He Loves loves loves loves loves "You"

"But whosoever drinketh of the water I shall give him shall never thirst; but the water that I shall give him shall be in him a well of water springing up into everlasting life" (John4: 14ᴋᴊᴠ)

And if it is everlasting, it is NOW

Glory Glory Glory Glory Glory to God!

Thank You Jesus! Thank You Holy Spirit! Thank You Father God! Amen.

Prayer for Salvation and Baptism in the Holy Spirit

The word of God says in Romans 10: "that if thou shalt confess with thy mouth the Lord Jesus, and shalt believe in thine heart that God hath raised him from the dead, thou shalt be saved. For with the heart man believeth unto righteousness; and with the mouth confession is made unto salvation. For the scripture saith, whosoever believeth on him shall not be ashamed." (Romans 10:9-11 KJV)

And in Romans 5 "But God commendeth his love toward us, in that, while we were yet sinners, Christ died for us Much more then, being now justified by his blood, we shall be saved from wrath through him." (Romans 5:8-9 KJV)

In John 3 "For God so loved the world that he gave his only begotten Son, that whosoever believeth in him should not perish, but have everlasting life." (John 3:16 KJV)

In 2 Corinthians 5 "Therefore if any man be in Christ, he is a new creature: old things are passed away; behold, all things are become new." (2 Corinthians 5:17 KJV)

In Acts 2 "And they were all filled with the Holy Ghost, and began to speak with other tongues, as the Spirit gave them utterance." (Acts 2: 4 KJV)

Dear Father God, Your word says, That if I call on the Name of the Lord I will be saved, and that if I confess with my mouth the Lord Jesus, and that I believe in my heart that you, have raised Him from the dead, I shall be saved. Heavenly Father I call on the Name of Jesus and I confess Jesus as Lord and believe in my heart that You Father God raised Him from the dead. I ask Jesus to come and live in me. I believe I am now Born Again a new creature in Christ, that I am a child of Almighty God. I ask You Father to fill me to overflowing with Your precious Holy Spirit, to come take residence up in me. Father God by faith I believe and praise Your Holy Name for my salvation and the indwelling of the Holy Spirit, with the evidence of speaking in other tongues. I expect to speak with other tongues as He; the Holy Spirit gives me utterance. Thank You my Lord and my Savior and Praise Your Holy Name, Blessing and Honor and Glory and Power forever. Amen

You Are Fearfully and Wonderfully Made

In the beginning God created the heavens and the earth. So God created man in His own image, in the image of God created He him; male and female created He them. And God saw everything that He had made, and, behold, it was very good. And evening and morning were the sixth day. Thus the heavens and the earth were finished and all the host of them. And God blessed the seventh day and sanctified it: because that in it He had rested from all His work which God created and made.

You have been created from the very beginning from God Himself.

God created you in the very beginning of creation. Not at your birth or conception. When God created and made the heavens and the earth and its entire host, your substance you, yet not formed, yet in God's book all of your members were written. Praise God. You were on the mind of God at the very creation. It was not by chance or mistake you were made. God created and wanted you. Hold tight to that knowledge, you are loved of your Heavenly Father and He wants you. He formed; He fashioned or grew together your being in your mother's womb. You are wonderfully put together, you were on the mind of God in the beginning and there after you were in His thoughts. He knows the thoughts that He thinks toward you. The thoughts and plans, plans of peace that are not evil, to give you an expected end. Good plans!

You are also fearfully and wonderfully made. Wonderfully put together and God saw everything He made and said "it is very good."

God Himself, behold you. The word behold here in Hebrew is hinneh – look! God looked at you and said it was very good!

Fearfully that your soul knows right well, We all have that measure of faith, confidence in God our Heavenly Father, that is what the enemy wants to steal from you so that he can place doubt dislike, low self-esteem, hurt and lies in your heart. Don't let him. Keep your eyes on the One who loves you, who wanted you always, from the very beginning, from before time. For God so loved you that gave His only begotten Son, that whosoever believes in Him should not perish, but have everlasting life. For God sent not His Son unto you to condemn you; but that you through Him you might be saved. That you would have life and that you have it more abundantly. Glory to God! Now that is very good news Adams sin brought death CHRIST gives us Life eternal

"In the beginning God created the heaven and the earth, "(Genesis 1:1KJV)"So God created man in his own image, in the image of God created he him; male and female created he them." (Genesis 1: 27 KJV) "And God saw everything that he had made, and, behold, it was very good. And the evening and the morning were the sixth day."(Genesis 1:31 KJV) "Thus the heavens and the earth were finished, and all the host of them." (Genesis 2:1 KJV) "And on the seventh day God ended his work which he had made; and he rested on the seventh day from all his work which he had made." (Genesis 2:2KJV)

> For thou hast possessed my reins: thou hast covered me in my mother's womb. I will praise thee; for I am fearfully and wonderfully made: marvelous are thy works; and that my soul knoweth right well. My substance was not hid from thee, when I was made in secret, and curiously wrought in the lowest parts of the earth. Thine eyes did see my substance, yet being unperfect; and in thy book all my members were written, which in continuance were fashioned, when as yet there was none of them.
>
> (Psalm 139:13-16 KJV)

"And all that dwell upon the earth shall worship him, whose names are not written in the book of life of the Lamb slain from the foundation of the world." (Rev 13: 8 KJV)

"For I know the thoughts that I think toward you, saith the LORD, thoughts of peace, and not of evil, to give you an expected end" (Jeremiah 29:11 KJV)

"For I say, through the grace given unto me, to every man that is among you, not to think of himself more highly than he ought to think; but to think soberly, according as God hath dealt to every man the measure of faith." (Romans 12:3 KJV)

"For God so loved the world, that he gave his only begotten Son, that whosoever believeth in him should not perish, but have everlasting life. For God sent not his Son into the world to condemn the world; but that the world through him might be saved." (John 3:16 KJV)

"The thief cometh not, but for to steal, and to kill, and to destroy: I am come that they might have life, and that they might have it more abundantly. I am the good shepherd: the good shepherd giveth his life for the sheep." (John 10:10-11 KJV)

Look this up in your Bible, read it for yourself in your own Bible, start marking scriptures that you receive from revolution of the Holy Spirit; and start on the ride of a lifetime, you will be so joyous and grateful to God you did.

Rom.10:8-13 Rom.3:23 Rom.5:8 Jojn3:16-18 Isa. 53:4-6 Eph.6:10-24 Eph.1:17-23 Heb. 4:7-16

The choice is always yours. As for me and my house we will serve the Lord!

May the Revelation of Jesus Christ come to you! Amen

Indi Fratarcangelo Kimsey is an author, minister, and evangelist who believes in and teaches the Good News for mankind, the word of God.

Indi has ministered to children, young adults, and families to bring hope to seemingly hopeless situations, encouragement to the troubled and weary, and God's truth to overcome life's difficulties. Indi has worked for several years in the prison and jail ministry.

It was through her reaching out and caring for others, she received what God revealed in her own heart, a new and deeper understanding about how his love, power, and strength can overcome all of life's challenges and provide the abundance of his promise for us all.

Indi was born and raised in upstate New York but now calls Florida home where she lives with her husband. She is blessed with a blended family of eight beautiful grown children, and seven incredible grandchildren, who bring new meaning to eight, is enough.

Indi accepted Jesus Christ as her Lord and Savior in late 1976, and was water baptized January 9, 1977 in the Atlantic Ocean off the coast of Jacksonville Florida.

*** Check out her website at *www.GodnamedJesus.com*

Or email her at *indi@godnamedjesus.com*

> "If you have ever wondered what it would be like to interview our Lord Jesus Christ concerning his purpose in coming to this earth, now is your chance. Indi uses the scriptures to reveal the thought life of God and Christ in the eternal plan of redemption. From the very beginning A Man-God Named Jesus was so interesting that I found myself eagerly turning the pages for her next thought."

Rev. Julian C. Walker, ThB, D.D.
Pastor
Family Worship Center